D1486504

Library of Congress Cataloging-in-Publication Data:

Names: McLeary, Susan, author. | Dumouchelle, Amanda, photographer
Title: The art of wearable flowers / Susan McLeary ; photographs by
    Amanda Dumouchelle.
Description: San Francisco : Chronicle Books, [2020] | Includes index.
Identifiers: LCCN 2019015726 | ISBN 9781452175874 (hardcover : alk. paper)
Subjects: LCSH: Floral decorations. | Dress accessories
Classification: LCC SB449.48 .M35 2020 | DDC 745.92--dc23 LC record
    available at https://lccn.loc.gov/2019015726

Manufactured in China.

Design by Vanessa Dina.
Typsetting by Howie Severson.

Photographs by Amanda Dumouchelle.

10 9 8 7 6 5 4 3 2 1

Chronicle Books LLC
680 Second Street
San Francisco, CA 94107
www.chroniclebooks.com

THE ART OF
Wearable Flowers

To my children, Leda and Maceo,
and to all the flower lovers that hold this
book in their hands: in floristry as in life—
create that which you crave to see.

THE ART OF
WEARABLE FLOWERS

Floral rings, bracelets, earrings, necklaces, and more

SUSAN MCLEARY

PHOTOGRAPHS BY
Amanda Dumouchelle

CHRONICLE BOOKS
SAN FRANCISCO

AN INSATIABLE PASSION

Many of us know Susan McLeary as "Passionflower Sue," the Instagram handle she adopted for her Ann Arbor, Michigan–based studio, originally named after the tropical vine *Passiflora caerulea*.

"Passion" is a fitting adjective for Sue, and I am reminded of my favorite garden quote from Karel Čapek's *The Gardener's Year*, published in 1929: "Let no one think that real gardening is a bucolic and meditative occupation. It is an insatiable passion, like everything else to which [we give our] heart."

Indeed, the generous creative whose book you hold in your hands has given over her heart to the practice of making beauty informed by botany.

I first met Sue in 2014 at a Chapel Designers' conference in New York City when founder Holly Chapple invited me to speak about the Slow Flowers movement. Susan brought a few of her intricate succulent jewelry pieces to share at the event, and I was immediately mesmerized by them. Like Susan, I was a bit of a fashionista, having earned my undergraduate degree in textiles and clothing and worked at *Seventeen* magazine as a junior editor in my early years after college.

Our friendship was forged, and the following year we reconnected at Lisa Waud's Detroit Flower Week, where Sue led a design team to transform an elderly kitchen into a fantasy floral setting that enchanted thousands of visitors over the three-day exhibition. That's when I first interviewed Sue for an episode of my *Slow Flowers* podcast.

In 2016, I asked Sue if she would accept a commission to create a signature headpiece for the second annual American Flowers Week, a Slow Flowers campaign. She jumped right into the assignment, designing a red-white-and-blue flower 'fro using all domestic US-grown flowers. Modeled by Monique Montri and photographed by Amanda Dumouchelle, the powerfully feminine piece symbolized all that I dreamed for the flower promotion campaign—and images from that project continue to be posted and shared to this day. (You can learn to make your own flower 'fro on page 185.)

Sue's personal belief that artists, designers, and florists must create the art they want to see in the world has made a great impression on me and on tens of thousands of her followers. In early 2017, I had just begun to contribute articles to *Florists' Review* magazine, and the "Creativity" issue was scheduled for March 2017. Travis

Rigby, the magazine's new owner and publisher, asked me for suggestions, and I blurted out: "Let's profile Susan McLeary on her creative process."

By then, Sue had a significant fan base on social media and as a design teacher, especially for her unique floral wearables and succulent jewelry. And while her work had been published in European floral publications, the "mainstream" floral marketplace hadn't fully discovered her incredible artistic talents. I'm so pleased that Travis and editor David Coake agreed to my proposed profile of Sue.

We recorded the interview when she came to my hometown to teach a wearable jewelry workshop for the Seattle Wholesale Growers Market. And in true Susan McLeary fashion, rather than providing a photo gallery of her past design work to accompany my story, she conjured up an entirely new body of wearable pieces, featuring a new palette, new flowers, and new shapes. She again collaborated with photographer-partner Amanda Dumouchelle to present fresh, modern fashion and flower-forward wearables to *Florists' Review* readers. We titled the article "A Curious Creative," and the ten-page spread featured exciting, convention-breaking looks, including a crescent bouquet, a floral bib, a three-way floral sash, and a dramatic, Cleopatra-style headdress. Sue wanted the images to reflect her philosophy that one must create and design in response to what one craves to see in the marketplace.

Her urge to share continues, and it is my desire that you will be entirely delighted with Sue's inventive and intricate approach to making floral couture accessories, jewelry, and wearable pieces. *The Art of Wearable Flowers* reveals her truly contagious passion on every page.

Sue's practice of openly sharing ideas and skills follows the advice she expressed to my readers in that *Florists' Review* article: "It feels so much better when you let your creativity out into the world. I believe that if you do this, more will return to you. If you hold it in, you're holding so tight that you can't absorb new information."

The greatest reward Sue will receive from having produced this magical and inventive book, into which she has poured years of experience in passionately satisfying her artistic curiosity, is to see you take these projects and concepts and make them your own. Use the techniques, methods, and advice; the designer secrets, proven tips, and lessons learned—and give yourself permission to aspire and elevate botanical wearables to reflect your own personality and imagination.

May the spirit of creativity and curiosity found in these pages be infectious—and send you on your own passionate journey. It will be a joyous and satisfying one.

—DEBRA PRINZING
Founder and creative director
of Slow Flowers Society
slowflowerssociety.com

INTRODUCTION:
MY FLORAL JOURNEY

I was a late bloomer when it came to floral design (pardon the pun). I've always been vaguely creative; I can remember spending hours on end as a child, sketching, beading, building elaborate fairy villages in the woods outside my home, and creating doll clothing. As a teen, I became obsessed with fashion and turned magazine cuttings from *Vogue*, *Elle*, and *W* into an enormous collage that covered my bedroom walls. I pored over these magazines, studying the haute couture work of revolutionary designers such as Jean Paul Gaultier, Thierry Mugler, and Christian Lacroix. But although I could be utterly consumed with a given creative obsession, I never pursued any of them seriously enough to imagine that one day I'd have a career in the arts. It was entirely by chance that I found this work.

After many years spent traveling, working as a line cook, waitress, and restaurant manager, and halfheartedly exploring possible careers—chef and physical therapist being the most promising prospects—I found myself back in my hometown of Ann Arbor, Michigan, finishing a bachelor of science degree and making jewelry for friends and for sale at a local boutique. I was in my late twenties, and many of my friends and acquaintances were getting married. Word of my jewelry-making hobby got out, and I started to receive requests to create jewelry pieces for local weddings. One friend asked me to make jewelry for herself and her bridesmaids, and as we talked, she confided that she hadn't yet hired a florist. Her wedding was just a few months away, and it was clear she was concerned about this missing detail. I can still recall her exact words as she grasped my arm and asked me if I would be her florist: "You're creative; you can probably do this!"

I agreed to design for her wedding, thinking it would be an interesting challenge, but I was not overly excited by the idea. It wasn't until I held her flowers in my hands that I recognized a transformation occurring inside me. My fingernails were stained black from the toil, I hadn't properly slept or eaten in days, I was absolutely exhausted, and the work had turned my kitchen into a veritable compost pile, but I had a permanent grin on my face, as I completely connected with the medium of flowers. I'd accidentally found a new creative obsession, and I recognized that this feeling deserved proper exploration. I felt a strong compulsion to envelop myself in the world of floral design. So I tucked all of my jewelry-making supplies away and dedicated myself fully to exploring this new passion.

Just as word of my jewelry hobby had spread, so did word of my floral design hobby. And as more of my friends married, I designed their wedding flowers, gifting my labor as a wedding present. As my passion grew, I sought out every learning opportunity. I read every floral design book I could get my hands on at my local library, watched every video I could find, and took every class I could afford. I earned a certification through the Michigan Floral Association, and through that program I found my first mentor, Dorota Knobloch. When I happened upon her work, I saw that floral design could be incredibly artful, imaginative, evocative, and expressive—just like the work of the couture fashion designers I'd admired all of my life. Her work further stoked my curiosity, and I realized that in order to grow, I needed to find full-time work as a florist to immerse myself in this craft. I left the restaurant job that had been my comfortable nest for more than a decade and found work in a bustling floral shop. There I designed for every kind of occasion, including everyday, funerals, and plenty of weddings and events. The experience gave me much-needed skills and confidence, but after a few years of floral shop work, my curious and restless nature tugged at me once more, and I felt the need to move forward. It was then that my own studio, Passionflower, was born.

The name for my studio was inspired by an experience I had during a trip to southern Italy with my now husband. I happened upon a passionflower vine growing on a stone wall, and it was the first time in my adult life that I was completely captivated by a flower. The passionflower plant is fascinating—with its multicolored petals and sepals, its incredibly ornate and intricately colored radial filaments, and its swirling, reaching tendrils that seem almost sentient. It absolutely mesmerized me, and there I was—entranced and frozen in the moment. I loved that this flower had the power to create pause. Each time I see a passionflower, a sort of calm washes over me and I'm transported back to that sunny stone wall in southern Italy. I named my studio Passionflower because I wanted my designs to evoke that same feeling of fascination, curiosity, and pausing to appreciate the moment, here and now. I wanted to give people that visceral experience through my work.

I never could have predicted how transformative the next several years would be.

Work as an event florist can be exhilarating, but it is also mentally and physically exhausting. And it can be terribly isolating. As I plodded forward, often spending long hours working alone—sometimes with a fussy baby strapped to my back—I yearned for connection and growth.

As my studio gained traction, the task of producing weddings started to feel restrictive and repetitive. It no longer inspired me, and I wasn't sure if my work was speaking to others in the way I initially intended. My insatiable curiosity pushed me to want to learn more. I wanted to continue to grow and move in a more artful direction, so I dove further into the floral world online and discovered a virtual constellation of inspiration. Incredibly artistic florists with passion equal to mine were out there—all I had to do was reach out and connect!

And connect I did. In 2013, I won a seat in one of floral couture florist Françoise Weeks's workshops. I'd admired her work online for years. Her impossibly detailed, supernatural work spoke with a voice uniquely hers. In the quiet of her studio, I was encouraged to explore until my own creative voice was audible—something I desperately wanted at that time. I returned home invigorated and determined to create floral art representative of my love for nature and floral design.

Shortly after returning home from this transformational workshop, I was asked to create floral jewelry for a photo shoot taking place in California. While I was designing for that shoot, it finally clicked in my mind that I could fuse my longtime love of fashion and jewelry design with my current floral obsession.

When I saw the photos from that shoot, I realized I was on to something very exciting. Not only did the work inspire me, but the reaction from the public was overwhelmingly positive and encouraging. I dusted off my jewelry-making supplies and, with renewed focus, shifted my energy toward creating wearable floral

art. I realized that if I focused on creating work that spoke to me, it would also speak to others. The more "myself" I was as a designer, the greater the reaction I received. This wonderful metamorphosis opened a floodgate of inspiration, and I've been caught in that current ever since.

As I practiced using my creative voice, I started to gain artistic clarity and confidence, and I began to connect with like-minded florists and photographers around the world. I shared my ideas and passion with them, and they with me, and these interactions resulted in numerous opportunities to teach, travel, collaborate, innovate, and share. One of these vital collaborations is with photographer Amanda Dumouchelle, whose gorgeous photographs fill this book. My work with Amanda has been instrumental in allowing me to show the world the work I want to make—instead of waiting for the world to ask me to make it! Her art has given life to mine, and I'm so grateful for the places it's taken me.

I share this book with the hope that the art of floral design inspires you as it has me; that the projects presented here beckon you to slow down, to marvel at the ephemeral beauty of nature. With this book, my full journey is realized— from fashion-obsessed dreamer to floral instructor and artist. I've shed my studio name, and no longer focus on weddings (although I've retained and use the nickname "Passionflower Sue" for Instagram and my online class website); instead,

I share what I've learned over the years in an effort to do my part in pushing floral artistry forward. I encourage you to be fearless and experimental in your own work, borrow from the lessons here, create that which you crave to see, and cultivate your own artistic voice. And I encourage you to carefully document your floral art and share it widely—you never know what opportunities may arise from it!

The projects in this book are organized by type of wearable, from simple floral jewels to elaborate headpieces—and so much more. Each project includes step-by-step instructions and photos and a list of the ingredients I've used for the design; feel free to substitute your own favorites or experiment with materials you find in your garden or at the local market. Many of these projects may look complex, but they are designed to be approachable even for a novice. I've also sprinkled bonus photos of wearable designs through-out the book, which I hope will further inspire your creations. It's my goal to empower all—flower enthusiasts, gardeners, fashionistas, novice designers, dreamers, and seasoned florists—to create wearable floral art that stokes wonder, curiosity, and an appreciation for the beauty of nature.

TOOLS AND TECHNIQUES

Floral design, much like cooking, is at once entirely approachable and frustratingly intimidating. It is my goal with this book to provide foundational tools, techniques, and principles of floral design that will give you the resources to explore the richness in this medium and completely fall in love with floristry as I have. In this section, you'll find notes on sourcing ingredients, essential tools, design tips, and more, so that you have the building blocks to successfully create the projects in later chapters and your own artful designs. It's my hope that the following pages answer questions, provoke thought and further study, and pique your interest into this satisfying work so that you continue to experiment with this ephemeral art form.

SOURCING

The task of sourcing floral ingredients can be time-consuming, challenging, crazy-making, and—when you do track down the perfect ingredients—utterly satisfying. The success of a given design depends greatly on the careful selection of the materials—their freshness, coloration, and size are all of great importance. Just as a conscientious chef must seek out the best sources for a recipe's ingredients, the florist must also search for the finest growers and markets that can reliably supply interesting, high-quality blooms. I spent years working in restaurants prior to my floral career, and I've noticed parallels between the worlds of

food and of flowers. The best restaurants create dishes representative of the season, sourcing locally as much as possible; they realize that this is how the medium of food can communicate a sense of place and time. When done well, this creates engaging dishes that spark memories, delight all the senses, and help sustain a vibrant local food economy. I believe this is a valuable goal for florists as well. And thanks to today's Slow Flowers movement, people are becoming more aware of the importance of sourcing flowers locally from sustainable sources.

Although I source flowers from all over the world, my search for materials always begins in my own backyard and expands outward from there. I live in the northern United States, and we have a short growing season and somewhat limited availability, so I've had to become a savvy sourcer. During the growing season, I buy as much as I can from local flower farms. We are lucky to have a wonderful weekly farmers' market, a local flower growers' cooperative, and numerous local greenhouses. I encourage you to explore your own location, find your best local sources, and frequent them. Get to know the growers, and help them get to know you—the relationships you forge will benefit you both. Most of the growers I buy from ask me what flowers I'm interested in, then offer to grow them—what could be better? In addition to local farms, numerous flower growers in other states will ship cut flowers. Many have a passion for a specific family of flowers—say, heirloom roses—and with advance notice will ship freshly cut flowers via overnight air.

In addition to investigating your regional options, look into buying from wholesale flower markets. In the United States, proper licensing is often required to shop at these markets, so prepare appropriately by doing some research ahead of time. A good wholesale market is a wonderful place to learn about flowers. Botanical materials gathered from near and far are offered for purchase. Some, like the cluster of markets on Twenty-Eighth Street in New York City or the San Francisco Flower Mart, have a dizzying array of delights on display for purchase. Those in smaller towns may have more limited offerings, but all floral wholesale markets allow you to place advance orders, which florists typically do when planning events. When you open an account with a wholesale market, you will be given a sales rep to work with—consider this person a valuable member of your design team. A good sales rep will quickly learn your preferences, and because they are acting as your eyes and ears, they can make recommendations for materials that will elevate your work.

Sourcing can be time-consuming, as there are many wonderful sources for materials, each with their own strengths. I've listed some of my favorite flower sources in the "Resources" section on page 218. Time spent learning about your options—from local to global—will broaden your palette and connect you to the sources of inspiring ingredients throughout the year.

SELECTION

When I met and fell in love with floristry, I became curious to learn as much as I could about the people, techniques, and design process of this world. Some years later, when I became interested in floral wearables, a new sort of curiosity was born (an obsession, really): to know the out-of-water longevity of every possible flower, foliage, blade, and berry. In my floral work up until that point, most materials I used were arranged directly into water, so their longevity wasn't paramount. I did have a go-to list of reliable flowers for making crowns, boutonnieres, and corsages, but my list really began to grow after I became obsessed with floral fashion and wearables. Ideally, the ingredients in floral wearables have the strength to last the length of the event they're intended for. Longevity and durability are important to the success of a given design. My list of reliables, gathered over the years by observation and testing, is my artist's palette—an ingredient list that I delight in adding to and look to for inspiration. I encourage you to borrow from the list I've gathered, observing the work of others—watching what materials they're using and in what season—and adding your tested favorites to grow your own list. Test materials as often as you can—the fallen bloom from a hanging pot of begonia, a hellebore snipped from the garden, a stem from the potted kalanchoe picked up at the grocer. The more you test, the broader and more exciting your palette becomes.

When making selections, in addition to the longevity and durability of materials, I also consider the form, color, size, and texture of materials. The choices you make with these design elements will allow you to convey (or conjure) emotion with your work—the true goal and definition of art!

Form

Form, or the physical shape of floral elements, is an important consideration when planning a design. The choice to use rounded ranunculus, garden rose, or peony in a design can create feelings of calm, romance, and softness, while choosing to use angular feather celosia, spiky thistle, or rigid, pointed kochia can create feelings of energy, excitement, and strength. Choosing to focus on one form within a design, and repeating it with all your material selections, creates unity in the piece; choosing to combine different forms within a piece creates contrast. You must also consider the entire form of the composition. When attempting to create a piece with a distinct geometric shape intended to create impact, such as the dome hat on page 181, you'll need to take extra care with perfecting the intended shape. It's essential to know what overall form you intend to create before starting the design process—this will inform all of your material selections.

Color

Color is arguably the design element with the greatest impact. It is the first thing we notice about a piece, and it most certainly influences our feelings about it. Put simply, warm colors excite and energize, and cool colors calm and soothe. Even if the forms in a piece are rounded and soft, such as garden roses or peonies, if they are vibrant red or bright yellow, they'll convey a dynamic, energetic message.

Conversely, if an angular material such as feather celosia or ginger is the design focus, the artist can still convey a message of calm and softness by choosing to use pastel pink celosia or white ginger instead of the electric red and orange shades also available. I tend to gravitate toward cool hues, as I look to plants to calm me and soften my mood. This preference often guides my color selections, but it doesn't prevent me from admiring bright colors in others' work and playing with bright color on occasion. I encourage you to observe your surroundings—your home decor, clothing, jewelry, and the art you gravitate toward—and I'm certain you'll see a pattern of color preference emerge. Allow this leaning to contribute to your unique aesthetic—I believe it lends personality to your work and should be embraced! In addition to the emotions colors convey on their own, color harmonies—the relationship between colors in a design—can communicate their own messages. I recommend becoming familiar with the twelve-spoke color wheel and diving into the myriad ways color can be combined.

There are twelve distinct color harmonies, nicely outlined in the American Institute of Floral Designers' *AIFD Guide to Floral Design*—an essential text for any florist; of these, the five that I see most frequently used in floral design are *monochromatic, analogous, complementary, split complementary,* and *polychromatic.*

Monochromatic color harmonies, as the name implies, are single-hue color schemes. Monochromatic pieces can contain many shades, tones, or tints of that hue, but all are values of the chosen color. (See page 181 for an example of a monochromatic color scheme.) Analogous harmonies contain three to five colors that occur next to each other on the color wheel. I often choose to play within an analogous color scheme, especially when venturing into brighter hues. I choose a three- to five-color "wedge" from the color wheel—for instance, red, red-orange, orange, yellow-orange, and yellow—and layer my design with many floral representations of those hues. I find that hot colors can inadvertently conjure a certain garish quality, and I believe this is softened by adding multiple color variations within the chosen color wedge. When this is done well, the color scheme gains a certain sophistication and calm quality. See page 207 for an example of an analogous color harmony. Ariella Chezar is a great example of a florist who works with vibrant color expertly—with refined, cohesive results.

Complementary color harmonies comprise a pair of hues situated directly across from each other on the color wheel. Combining colors from opposite sides of the wheel creates a color interaction that innately appeals to humans and a dynamic, energetic composition. An often-seen variation to this harmony, near-complementary color harmony, is achieved when a given color is paired with a color that lies next to its direct opposite. The headpiece on page 171 shows this color harmony—pairing red with yellow-green instead of true green, red's direct complement.

Another common harmony is the analogous-complementary color harmony, created by adding the two adjacent colors on either side of one of the colors in the complementary pair. The necklace on page 55 shows this harmony—varying shades of purple are paired with purple's direct complement, yellow, and layered with yellow-green and true green. Split-complementary color harmonies are created by combining a color with the two colors that lie on either side of its direct opposite. An example of a split-complementary color scheme is the combination of red with blue-green and yellow-green. All the complementary schemes are best executed by adding many varying representations of the chosen colors. Bicolor blooms, such as yellow and purple pansies, are designer gold—they can be used to instantly marry two complementary colors within a scheme.

The last of the five harmonies that I often see is the polychromatic color harmony. "Poly," meaning "many," describes this harmony, comprising many otherwise unassociated colors. This can be seen in Dutch masters' paintings, in the wonderful work of Anne ten Donkelaar, and in the exuberant floral art of Azuma Makoto. In addition to familiarizing yourself with the twelve-spoke color wheel and its many harmonies, I recommend consulting a comprehensive color wheel and having one present in your workspace. My favorite is the quirky "Martian Colour Wheel" created by Warren Mars. The wheel is very useful to florists, as it contains many shades, tones, and tints and has the added charm of color-true edible names such as "ham," "Parmesan cheese," "avocado," and "turmeric."

Size

It is important to consider both the size of the complete arrangement as well as the size of the individual ingredients within an arrangement before creating a design. Florists must continually consider size—it is truly crucial to the successful execution of every type of floral work, and it is essential when considering how to marry a floral piece to it is setting. It is most certainly important to the success of floral wearables. If a florist wants to create a delicate, light, ethereal piece, selecting small blooms will carry this feeling into the piece, whereas choosing large, heavy blooms will weigh down the design and counteract the desired effect. When designing to accent a delicate part of the body—say the earlobes or fingers—the size of the floral material is paramount to the execution of the design. Petite, light materials will much better complement these body parts than large, heavy ones. Keep this in mind when making your floral selections or consider manipulating large materials to make them more suitable for pieces intended for petite places. For example, consider working with individual allium florets instead of the whole bloom head, or deconstructing a stem of delphinium and using the florets instead of the entire floral spike.

Texture

Texture—the surface appearance or physical qualities of natural materials—is another important element to consider when selecting ingredients for a given design, as textural choices can add richness and context and can also elicit emotions or spark associations for the viewer. A mix of diverse textures can create contrast or tension in a piece; choosing one texture and combining materials that all share that textural quality can create a more unified, cohesive piece. Materials that appear fuzzy, silky, or velvety can evoke comforting emotions, while rough or spiky materials can stir more challenging emotions.

Choosing to create floral wearables using ingredients that resemble commonly used clothing textiles, such as leather or velvet, can play to the viewers' associations with these familiar materials and add even more charm and surprise to the pieces. For instance, the slightly fuzzy undersides of thick magnolia leaves resemble rich, auburn suede, and the fine, downy nap of lamb's ear foliage resembles thick velveteen fabric. One could craft a winter muff out of lamb's ear or a pair of floral shoes out of leathery magnolia, creating an intriguing collision of the familiar and the unexpected.

HANDLING

All fresh flowers have a life span—a frustrating quality that challenges all of us, from grower, to designer, to consumer. In response, those of us on the front end of the process make decisions and perform care rituals to make the most of each bloom. When creating floral wearables, I rely on a long list of reliable materials that I have tested over the years. These reliable materials are ones that you can expect to last the length of an event, but they still require proper handling upon receipt to perform at their best.

I typically make sure to have my flowers on hand two to three days before I intend to present them, to allow enough time to process them appropriately. For example, if a floral headpiece is requested for a Saturday event, I'll bring the flowers into the studio on Wednesday or Thursday. After they arrive, I clean their stems thoroughly, removing damaged petals and unnecessary or excessive foliage, cut the stems at an angle with sharp shears, and place them in clean buckets filled with cool water that has been treated with Floralife 200, a conditioner made for the floral trade that increases freshness and hydration. In addition, I use Quick Dip hydration solution for all field-grown flowers and woody-stemmed materials such as roses and hydrangea. I allow the flowers to rest and hydrate in their buckets for at least 3 to 4 hours before tucking them into the cooler.

I also love to design with more delicate blooms such as lilac, hosta, fritillaria, and hydrangea florets. For these less-reliable materials, I often employ an additional hydration step that I recently learned from master florists Gregor Lersch and Hitomi Gilliam. After these stems have had a good long room-temperature drink, I trim them all to the length I plan to use, and place them in a sealable container or bag that I've lined with damp paper towels. I lay

the flowers in a single layer on the towels, spray them with water, and then repeat with another layer of damp paper towels. I continue to layer until all my flowers are safely tucked in and then spray the inside of the container with water as well. I then secure the lid on the container and place it in my cooler. The container, which acts as a moisture chamber, can rest in the cooler for 24 to 48 hours. This step allows the flowers and foliage to "harden"—hydrating through the surface of their petals or leaves. Since I learned this method, I've used it on many notoriously delicate, wilt-prone flowers with wonderful results.

After the wearable pieces are designed, I spray them with water, tuck them into an airtight plastic box or bag (look for compostable plastic options online at food supply companies) that I've also spritzed with water, and place it in the cooler. The final (optional) step is to apply a finishing spray to the pieces. This is done right before the pieces are presented. This seals the surface of the piece, locking in the moisture I've worked hard to secure.

I often hear florists say that they make their wearable pieces at the very last moment before an event. If this is your method, I urge you to try the steps just outlined. Making them earlier allows for much more thorough hydration of the flowers and foliage. Instead of just hydrating through their stems, they hydrate through the pores in the surface of their petals and leaves, increasing their durability and life span.

I realize not everyone reading this is a professional florist with a cooler and access to (or interest in) all these floral trade potions. A dark, cool space such as a basement or barn also works well for storage in place of a floral cooler, and immaculately clean buckets and clean, cool water will certainly suffice—especially when you're using locally sourced, freshly cut flowers. And I've used my home refrigerator with success countless times over the years, though it's important to note that the ethylene gas released by ripening produce can shorten the life of flowers. If you plan to use your refrigerator to preserve your flowers, I recommend purchasing an ethylene absorber. Home refrigerators also often have very cold spots, which pose a possible freezing danger. Flowers will not bounce back after freezing, so get to know the zones of your refrigerator before using it to store a precious floral artwork.

I encourage you to try these tips and to test flowers and foliage incessantly! Soon you will have a process that works for you and a long list of reliable floral favorites of your own.

DESIGN PROCESS

When I first started as a florist, I had no real process—only a strong idea of what I wanted to create and a vague idea of how to arrange the components to reach the desired end. Sometimes the designs were successful; other times they weren't. I'd read about the principles of floral design (I encourage you to as well), but I didn't have a reliable system or set of guidelines of my own to use to put them into play. Through years of reading, observing others, creating, taking apart, and

creating again, I've developed some helpful rules based on a set of principles that I use over and over again. These design rules guide my work and lend a certain ease to my process, whether I'm working on a delicate pair of succulent earrings or a large-scale floral installation. When I'm stuck, I lean on them to solve my questions. If a design feels stiff, or forced, or too contrived, these rules help me edit the piece back to a better, more natural place.

Most of these rules are simple and intuitive, but worth outlining here, as they help create a streamlined system, and I've found them valuable to students who struggle with their own process. I share them here with the hope that they will be just as helpful to you.

Contrast

Unlike painting, where you can mix colors and create your own palette, flower colors cannot be easily changed. However, careful selection and thoughtful placement of flowers in a composition allow the designer to create cohesive, well-blended pieces. When combining colors in a piece, I typically work from darkest to lightest—placing the deepest tones first and layering lighter tones on top. This draws the eye into the design, creating depth in the piece. This is especially important when combining high-contrast materials—say, white and black flowers. Placing them side by side on the same plane would result in a spotted, polka-dotted appearance.

Weight

When it comes to the weight of materials, I typically work from heaviest to lightest and largest to smallest. Heavy, dangling, or large elements are added to the piece first, and each subsequent layer is added in order from most to least substantial.

Air

Air (or space, as florists refer to it) is its own layer—an important ingredient that is purposely maintained between the floral layers. This ensures that each layer is visible (to the extent that you choose as the designer), thereby creating depth—critical to a successful composition. Without depth, the design will be one-dimensional and static. I also think about leaving space around individual blooms, instead of placing them so closely that they appear forced or squeezed together. Giving each bloom its own space allows the eye to move freely within the piece, creating a naturally pleasing, effortless-looking composition.

The Golden Ratio

I've always appreciated naturalistic, uncontrived floral design—the kind seen in a Dutch masters painting or that looks plucked from the garden—and I've sought to reproduce that with my work. But it wasn't until a conversation with a very talented floral artist and friend, Joseph Massie, that I realized I achieve this by employing three design principles: the golden triangle, the rule of thirds, and "3-5-8." All these concepts are derived from the golden ratio—the fascinating mathematical concept that informs the structure of all natural things.

Joseph and I were chatting at a floral conference while I worked on a floral necklace. I placed the first layer of blooms—three roses of varying sizes—laying them in a triangular fashion on the necklace base: the largest bloom just to the left of center, a slightly smaller bloom about one-third of the way up the left side of the piece, and the smallest, a rosebud, on the right, nearly at the top of the necklace base. As Joseph watched me work, he asked if I knew why I was spacing the flowers as I was. I told him I wasn't exactly sure why, but that I work in triangles—placing floral components in my designs following a series of asymmetrical triangular placements. Each point of the triangle receives a different "serving size" of floral material, layer by layer, until the piece is complete. He told me that I'd been applying the principles of the golden ratio to my way of designing. Further exploration revealed that the proportional rule I used to allocate my materials is derived from the golden ratio rule of proportion, the triangular placement that I rely on comes from the principles of the golden triangle, and the choice to place my focal point off center can be traced to the compositional concept of the rule of thirds.

The golden ratio, 1:1.618—also called "phi"—is a mathematical concept, famously explained by the fifteenth-century mathematician Filius Bonacci. His "Fibonacci" number sequence is the mathematical representation of the proportional patterns observed in nature. Phi is the value that defines the relationship between the numbers in the sequence.

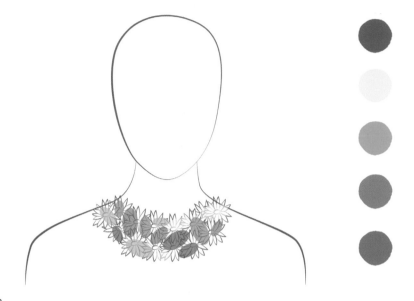

sequence 3-5-8

This "sacred geometry" can be observed in the natural structure of many things—from the number of petals of a flower, to the proportions of the leaf pattern of a succulent, to the spiral configuration of seeds in a head of a sunflower. The golden ratio offers a way to think about the proportional relationship among elements in a composition and shows that an innately pleasing natural balance is found in proportions that are carefully chosen to not be equal but to instead follow this pattern.

The sequence 3-5-8 is part of the Fibonacci number sequence; it is used to decide the relative quantities of each design element in a composition. The sequence should not be interpreted literally in terms of how many ingredients to use, but that ratio should help guide the appropriate relationship among the large, medium, and small amounts of a given element in a composition. Remember the three roses of varying size in my necklace story?

The largest rose represented the 8 in my design, the smaller rose the 5, and the rosebud the 3. Following this natural law of proportion will help you assign visual weight and allocate color throughout a piece, resulting in a naturally proportioned look.

The golden triangle is an isosceles triangle in which the sides are in golden proportion (phi) to the base. The triangular placements I'd been using in my work follow this concept. It's the relationship of the points in these triangles that has been the most helpful to me, especially informing my stem placements. For my students, awareness of this concept has been particularly helpful. When a piece is becoming too stiff, symmetrical, or static, the golden triangle can help illuminate what edits are necessary to coax the design back to a naturally pleasing, well-proportioned composition of elements.

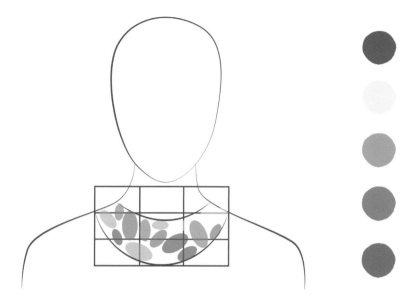

rule of thirds

The rule of thirds is another useful concept that designers use to choose where to place focal emphasis in a composition. It's most commonly applied in photography, painting, and filmmaking, and just as easily applied in floral design. Imagine that a composition is contained within a rectangle and divided into nine equally proportioned boxes. Two vertical lines and two horizontal lines make up the grid. If you're analyzing a photograph of a floral design, adjust the image so the very tips of the flowers are just contained within the frame, then apply the grid. The rule suggests that important focal elements are best placed along one of these lines—or where they intersect—to create compositions that draw the eye in and lead it throughout the piece. If multiple focal interest areas are placed along these lines, you can create a visual path for the eye to follow from point to point, resulting in a dynamic, rhythmic composition. You can choose to exaggerate these placements or play with them more subtly. If you instead place the focal point centrally and additional focal areas symmetrically, the resulting piece is much more static. The eye is drawn into the piece but stops, and the rhythmic quality and movement of the composition is dramatically reduced.

To bring all these concepts together, I visualize the overall shape or physical edges of the design I plan to create before I start arranging. This shape, which I call my "canvas," is the total space I have to work in. I choose a starting point and, borrowing from the compositional concept of the rule of thirds, I place my first, most substantial floral element. This will be my focal point—it can be composed of the largest bloom, the most vibrant color, or otherwise the most visually striking material. It is placed off center, often in the lower third of the piece. Shifting to

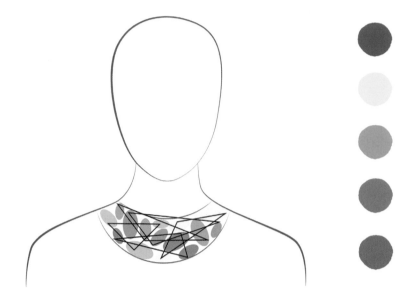

golden triangle

another of my core compositional concepts, I visualize this starting point as
one corner of the golden triangle, as well
as the 8 of a 3-5-8 sequence. I then position the other two corners in proportion
to the first and, using the 3-5-8 rule, place
my next-largest element at the far end of
the imaginary triangle, and the smallest
expression of that element at the third
and final corner, therefore assigning
visual weight to each corner of the triangle. With this first floral layer complete,
I then choose a blank space in the design
and repeat this triangular layout. I
repeat again and again, with all of my
floral layers, until my desired shape is
achieved and the piece satisfactorily filled.
(Note: Some designs don't benefit from
or require these steps—for example, the
purposefully static, uniform, single-
flower-type dome hat on page 181.)

Together, the golden triangle, 3-5-8, and
rule of thirds are visual concepts that
work with the classic principles of floral
design, specifically balance, proportion, dominance of one focal point, and
rhythm. Applying these concepts to your
work will immediately reward you with
a naturally pleasing composition. I also
encourage you to continually test and
push these concepts in your own work
and seek inspiration by analyzing the
work of other artists. Once you begin to
explore this infinitely rich source of inspiration, the well will never dry up!

ESSENTIAL TOOLS AND TECHNIQUES

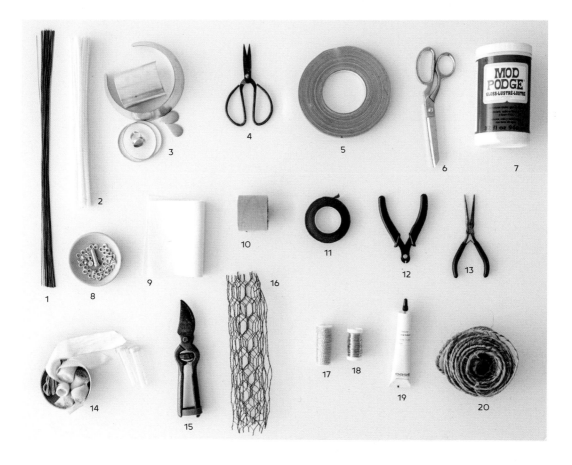

1. 24-gauge floral wire

2. Chenille stems
(pipe cleaners)

3. Assorted brass jewelry
blanks

4. Snips

5. Waterproof tape

6. Ribbon shears

7. Mod Podge craft gue

8. Eyelet kit

9. Faux leather fabric

10. Kinesiology tape
with a paper backing

11. Stem wrap tape

12. Wire cutters

13. Needle-nose pliers

14. Silk ribbons

15. Clippers

16. Florist's netting

17. Gold bullion wire

18. Gold jewelry wire

19. Oasis floral adhesive

20. Oasis rustic wire

WIRING TECHNIQUES

Wiring is an essential skill that allows designers to work with a wide array of materials and use individual blooms, leaves, or berries. Materials that have unreliable or bulky stems can be individually wired into designs. Wiring replaces the stem of the floral material with a slim but strong bendable wire, which gives the designer more control of the materials. Wired stems can defy gravity and create strong but light and airy designs. There are quite a few wiring techniques; following, I've described the four I use most frequently. When wiring, I typically work with 24- or 26-gauge floral wire, cut in half.

Piercing

Also called cross-piercing, this technique is best for flowers with sturdy stems, such as roses, lisianthus, and carnations. Using a 24-gauge floral wire, pierce the stem of the flower, just below the calyx. (For large or heavy blooms, insert another wire just below the first.) Bend the wire ends down to meet the natural stem, and trim the natural stem to about 1 in (2.5 cm) long. Tightly secure stem wrap just below the calyx, and pulling the tape taut, tape the entire length of the wire/stem bundle with the stem wrap.

Insertion

This method is best used with materials that have slim but durable stems and firm heads, such as scabiosa blooms and pods, berries, and strawflowers. Cut the stem of the floral material to about 1 in (2.5 cm) long. Place a 24- or 26-gauge floral wire next to the stem of the floral material, and insert one end into the bloom head. Grasp the natural stem and wire between your fingers, and firmly tape with stem wrap tape.

Cranking

This technique provides a reliable way to secure groupings of small florets, berries, herbs, or petals. I often wire clusters of carnation petals, grouped stems of privet, and agapanthus florets. Soft, fleshy stems must be gathered and wrapped in stem wrap tape first to prevent damage by the wire. Firm, leathery, or woody stems do not require pretaping. To wire, gather the bundle in one hand, fold a 24- or 26-gauge wire over the bundle just below the bloom head, grasp one end of the wire, and "crank" it around the bundle two or three times until it feels securely attached. Bring the two ends of the wire down, and wrap the entire "stem" with stem wrap tape.

Hook

This technique works wonderfully with disk-shaped and flat flowers, such as ranunculus, chrysanthemum, and firm, tightly structured succulents. To wire, first trim the stem of the floral material to about 1 in (2.5 cm) long. Next, bend one end of the wire to form a narrow "U" shape. Sink the long end of the wire into the bloom, and guide it down until the U-shaped portion meets the surface of the bloom. Lifting petals as needed, guide the shorter end of the wire through the surface of the bloom as well, until the U-shaped "hook" is fully embedded and disappears into the bloom head. Both ends of the wire will appear below the bloom head. Pinch the wires and stem together, and secure with stem wrap tape.

PIERCING METHOD

INSERTION METHOD   CRANKING METHOD

HOOK METHOD

WORKING WITH FLORAL ADHESIVE

It took me quite a few tries to get comfortable working with floral adhesive (sold as adhesive, but for brevity it is often called glue), but once I did, I realized the incredible freedom achieved with this tool. I use it so often, my close friends nicknamed me "Sue Glue." Indeed, it may sound silly, but I find this tool indispensable. Flowers are living things—fragile and often fleshy—with limited longevity. Attaching them with floral adhesive instead of wiring them or binding in place allows the designer to create dreamlike floral tapestries, quickly and securely. Here are a few important tips for working with floral glue:

- Keep the tube nozzle clean so the glue can run freely.

- Keep the tube upright when not in use.

- Add a fine layer of glue to the flower you plan to attach, as well as to the attachment point. Wait 10 to 15 seconds for both surfaces to get tacky, then press them together and hold until they are bonded.

- Work in a well-ventilated area or use a fan to blow fumes away from you as you work. This is especially important when working on multiple or large projects.

- Keep a little bowl nearby to use as a reservoir. Squeeze small amounts of glue into this bowl to dip materials into for efficiency and ease.

Consider glue as a method for adding the finishing touches to wired projects. Glue is perfect for adding delicate materials such as agapanthus or nerine florets that are otherwise difficult to wire.

FLORAL JEWELS MADE WITH JEWELRY BLANKS

Jewelry blanks are ready-to-use bases for crafting and jewelry design. I use brass jewelry blanks primarily, but they are also available in a variety of other materials, including aluminum, acrylic, shell, leather, vinyl, and wood. Florists are always on the hunt for the perfect vessel to display an arrangement of blooms, paying close attention to the color, form, size, and style. Ideally, the flowers and vessel become one cohesive display, each element aesthetically supporting the other. Jewelry bases are like vessels in that way; the platforms come in myriad shapes, sizes, and styles that you can use as little canvases to display a curated selection of flowers and foliage. These blanks are widely available, inexpensive, and easy to use, allowing the designer to make impressive floral accessories with ease. They are specifically created with durability and functionality in mind, making them ideal wearable vessels. In chapter 1, "Simple Floral Jewels" (page 35), I've outlined the steps to create your own wearable flowers using a variety of my favorite jewelry blanks.

FLORAL JEWELS MADE WITH FAUX LEATHER FABRIC

My discovery of faux leather as a base for floral jewelry happened quite by accident. I was asked to be part of a photo shoot, and after I made the required centerpieces and bouquets, I decided to make a few pieces of floral jewelry. I was determined to create a bib statement necklace, but I was short on time and unsure how to execute the vision I had in my mind. A hurried rummage through my junk jewelry drawer produced a bib-style necklace with a beaded appliqué that I'd long forgotten about. I peeled off the beaded facade, revealing a platform of sturdy faux leather fabric—the perfect base for attaching flowers! The floral design made quite an impact at the shoot, and the reaction I received encouraged me to experiment further. I realized I could easily and inexpensively create my own necklace and bracelet bases with faux leather—indeed, the design possibilities are limited only by the imagination!

Finding fabric for floral jewelry is easy. Most fabric stores stock the appropriate materials. Look for faux leather, also called "vegan leather" or pleather, and upholstery vinyl, sometimes called "marine vinyl." These fabrics, typically sold by the yard in standard widths of 45 or 60 in (110 or 150 cm), are inexpensive and easy to manipulate. The fabric is strong—durable enough to hold the weight of flowers—but feels light on the body and smooth against the skin.

To use fabric as a base, first sketch a template out of pattern paper or felt, cut it out, and test the template on yourself or a dress form. Once you're happy with the shape of your template, trace the template onto the fabric and cut out the base. Necklaces can be designed by cutting an oval "O" shape out of the fabric, with a large enough opening to simply slip over the head, or eyelets can easily be added to create attachment points for ribbon ties, or a chain and clasp. For bracelets, I usually add eyelets and ribbon to use to secure onto the wrist, but there is an even simpler solution—see the Petite Ribbon Corsage on page 103 for instructions.

CARING FOR FLORAL ARTWORK

One of the questions I'm most frequently asked about floral jewelry and wearables is "How long will that last?" This question always ruffles my feathers a bit, because I believe the ephemeral quality of flowers is one of their strengths. They captivate as they peak and then quickly fade, inviting us to pause and relish the beauty of the moment. This said, I do want the wearables I make to last through the duration of an event or party, and I expect them to look fresh for at least 6 hours. There are ways to improve the longevity of flowers and foliage, and I have tested these methods with great success. Please see "Handling" on page 20.

Proper conditioning is part of creating durable floral pieces, but you must also take care when packaging and presenting artworks. If you've made a piece that requires glue, after you're satisfied with the completed design, set it aside for at least 30 minutes to allow the glue to set.

After the piece has dried, spray with water to allow even more hydration through the surface of the petals and leaves. If storing for a later wear date, tuck the piece into an appropriately sized plastic bag, spritz the interior of the bag with water, and seal. If you're presenting the piece to a client or as a gift, tuck it into a lovely gift box or linen drawstring bag (I use brown paper boxes filled with shredded paper) and store in your cooler or refrigerator until presentation. I will often spray finished designs with a finishing spray such as Floralife Crowning Glory just before delivery. This gentle spray seals the surface of flowers and foliage, reducing moisture loss.

Many of the pieces in this book include succulents, and succulent jewelry pieces are simple to care for. Succulents are extremely resilient and last very well as mounted cuttings. Once made, the pieces will last 1 to 3 weeks without any special treatment. For best results, keep them out of extreme temperatures and direct light (sunlight won't harm them, but it will cause them to grow off their jewelry bases, resulting in leggy plants and a less tidy look). Succulents don't like to be too cold, so for cold climates like mine, I avoid making these during the winter months, as they aren't easily wearable outdoors.

Succulent jewelry pieces are perfect for special occasions such as a wedding, dance, birthday celebration, or Mother's Day gift—and after wear, they can be replanted as keepsake plants. Gently remove the plants from their jewelry setting and place on top of a 50/50 mix of organic potting soil and either perlite or sand. Rooting hormone can be used to speed the process along. I've made more than eight hundred succulent jewelry pieces over the years, and I've received quite a few photos of thriving potted plants in their owners' homes, months or years after their initial wear.

The first piece of floral jewelry I ever designed was a funky three-finger ring made during a 2013 workshop with the amazing floral couture designer Françoise Weeks. The experience was thrilling, as I realized that I could fuse my longtime love of jewelry making with my current floral obsession. Ideas flooded my head and filled my sketchbook, and I returned home from that workshop invigorated and full of inspiration.

Back in my studio, I was determined to create the pieces that I had in my imagination—sleek, detailed, flower-focused jewelry. I wanted viewers to marvel at the pieces and wonder how they were attached to their jewelry platforms. I began to experiment, testing many different ways to design the pieces. I retrieved my old jewelry kit from the basement and played with the techniques I'd used to make jewelry in the past, wiring and linking the flowers together. I also experimented with making my own decorative aluminum wire bases and even bought a soldering iron, which I used to bond metal jewelry findings together. Unfortunately, none of these methods gave me the clean, finished look I was after. But after much trial and error, I finally landed on two main ways to achieve the look I was going for: using premade jewelry blanks, and creating my own bases out of faux leather fabric. In the following pages, I'll share a number of my favorite projects using these methods, along with another surprisingly simple but effective method for attaching flowers directly to the skin.

FLORAL RING

If you're new to the world of floral jewelry, this is an ideal project to start with. Be sure to find a ring base with a bezel cup — the walled "plate" designed to hold a stone in place — as this little "tray" offers a perfect container in which to arrange and secure flowers and foliage — just like planting a miniature garden.

MATERIALS

- Bezel cup brass ring base
- Oasis floral adhesive
- Dried sheet moss
- Astrantia
- Cotinus fluff

- Honey garlic
  (*Allium siculum*)
- Immature blueberries
- Nigella 'African Bride'
- Tumbleweed onion
  (*Allium schubertii*)

STEP 1: Line the ring base with a thin layer of glue—just enough to lightly moisten the surface of the bezel cup. Wait 10 to 15 seconds to allow the glue to get tacky.

STEP 2: Press fine threads of moss into the glue.

STEP 3: After the moss is locked in place, add another fine layer of glue on top of the moss.

STEP 4: Trim flowers and foliage to the desired size, add a fine layer of glue to the largest bloom, and add it to the ring base, pressing firmly to ensure that it adheres to the base.

STEP 5: Continue to add your materials, layer by layer, from heaviest to lightest. Press each addition down onto the base firmly, holding the material in place for 10 to 15 seconds to make sure it adheres to the base. As you add material, play with depth by placing dark or large items closer to the jewelry base and lighter, more delicate, or more transparent items higher in the piece so that they float above to create dimension in the arrangement.

STEP 6: Finish with the most delicate or airy materials, leaving a bit of length on the stem to allow them to extend past the other ingredients so that they dance around the edges of the arrangement.

STUD EARRINGS

I was thrilled when I found stud earring bases with bezel cups—I love how this allows the flowers and foliage, not the jewelry bases, to be the sole focus of the design. Here, fern curls, kangaroo paw, coleus, and stunning clematis centers in jewel tones mingle, creating a pair of eye-catching earrings reminiscent of a pair of faux-gem clusters I rocked in the '90s. The gilded nigella foliage elevates the arrangement with a little extra shine.

MATERIALS:

- Oasis floral adhesive
- 1 pair bezel cup or flat-surfaced earring stud bases
- Dried sheet moss
- Uhele fern curls
- Kangaroo paw
- Coleus foliage
- Clematis blooms, petals removed
- Nigella 'African Bride'
- Design Master gold spray paint

STEP 1: Apply a thin layer of glue to the stud earring bases.

STEP 2: Press fine threads of moss onto the glued portion of each base. After the moss is locked in place, add another fine layer of glue on top of the moss.

STEP 3: Remove the stems from the fern curls, and trim to the desired size (I trimmed my curls until they were about ½ in [12 mm] across), then apply a fine layer of glue to their undersides, and press them onto the earring bases. Next, choose petite kangaroo paw blooms (the ones here are also about ½ in [12 mm] long), add glue, and press down onto the base next to the fern curls. Cut 2 petite coleus leaves from their stems, add glue, and tuck them into the design, opposite the kangaroo paw. Next add the clematis centers. Trim their stems flush, add glue to the underside, and press down between the fern curls and kangaroo paw, allowing them to "float" a little higher over the other materials.

STEP 4: Remove the petals from the nigella blooms and spray the sepals with the gold paint. Allow them to dry for a few minutes, cut them from the bloom, and glue them to the composition. Tuck them into the center of the piece, angling them so they appear to float over the edge. With each addition, press down onto the base firmly, holding for 10 to 15 seconds to make sure each has adhered to the base.

HYACINTH HOOPS

This simple project yields an incredibly striking result. Two ingredients and 10 minutes is all it takes to create these hoops for yourself. Hyacinth blooms are the perfect material for this design, as they are widely available, and the blooms nest together so beautifully on the earring, but other tubular or bell-shaped florets such as stephanotis, tuberose, and Persian lily (*Fritillaria persica*) would be lovely as well.

MATERIALS:

• Hyacinth pips

• 1 pair continuous
  hoop earrings

STEP 1: Snip the hyacinth pips off of their stem, choosing blooms of a similar size.

STEP 2: Thread the pips onto the earring by piercing the base of the flowers with one end of the open hoop, threading them onto the earring, and pulling them all the way to the end of the hoop.

STEP 3: Continue to thread blooms onto the hoop until fully covered.

DANGLY EARRINGS

I love making and wearing dangly earrings — the longer, the better! I've shown a more reserved arrangement here, but don't feel confined by the border of the brass bases; you can attach cascading materials to the very edge of the platforms for even more extension. If you want to play with other ingredients, pendulous flowers such as hanging amaranthus, *Pieris japonica*, feather, acacia, lily of the valley, and fuchsia would be gorgeous in this application.

MATERIALS:

- Needle-nose jewelry pliers
- 1 pair french hook ear wires
- 1 pair ¾ in (2 cm) long pear-shaped brass drops with holes
- Oasis floral adhesive

- Dried sheet moss
- Astrantia
- Tumbleweed onion (*Allium schubertii*)
- Honey garlic (*Allium siculum*)
- Immature blueberry

- Lilac, preconditioned (see "Handling" on page 20)
- Nigella 'African Bride'
- Cotinus blooms

STEP 1: Using jewelry pliers, gently open the attachment loop of the ear wires, feed the brass drops on, and pinch the loops to close.

STEP 2: Apply a thin layer of glue to the earring bases, and press fine threads of moss onto them.

STEP 3: After the moss is glued in place, add another fine layer of glue on top of the moss.

STEP 4: Trim the astrantia blooms as you like; I trimmed them in half to be able to use the bloom, while also saving room on the brass drop for my other floral materials.

STEP 5: Add glue to the backs of the astrantia blooms and press them firmly onto the earring base.

STEP 6: Add the alliums, blueberries, lilac, nigella florets, and cotinus. With each addition, press down onto the base firmly, holding the material in place for 15 to 20 seconds to make sure each has adhered to the base.

STATEMENT NECKLACE

This satisfying project is easy to make, and the result is in an impressive, showstopping piece of floral couture. Faux leather fabric is the ideal material to use for this. I suggest buying extra so that you can experiment with creating your own necklace templates. The design I'm sharing here is quite tailored—I've chosen to "color inside the lines" by placing all my materials within the edges of the template, but you shouldn't feel bound to the borders of the template. The fabric is quite strong, and materials can extend beyond the edge of the template, adding even more drama, drape, or tassel effect.

MATERIALS:

- Necklace template (see "Sourcing" on page 16)
- Faux leather fabric
- Eyelet kit
- Silk ribbon
- Oasis floral adhesive
- 12 to 15 stems *Fritillaria uva-vulpis*

- 10 to 12 stems heuchera foliage
- 10 to 15 stems kangaroo paw
- 20 to 25 stems muscari
- 1 or 2 stems Persian lily (*Fritillaria persica*)

- 2 or 3 stems *Pieris japonica*
- 3 to 5 stems snowberry (*symphoricarpos*)
- 2 or 3 stems tuberose

STEP 1: Using a necklace template, trace out your design on your fabric. For this project, I used the template available on my website (susanmcleary.com) to create a cardboard template. I encourage you to experiment with creating your own templates. First use felt or pattern paper to sketch out your desired design, then test it on a dress form or on yourself to make sure it works before cutting it out of fabric.

STEP 2: Cut your necklace base out of the fabric.

STEP 3: Following the instructions on the kit, add eyelets to either side of the necklace base.

STEP 4: Thread ribbon or cord of your choice through each eyelet.

STEP 5: Prepare the base by adding a fine layer of glue to the unfinished surface—most faux leather and upholstery fabrics have one finished and one unfinished side. Make sure to add your flowers and foliage to the unfinished side; the smooth, finished side should be the one that rests against the wearer's skin.

STEP 6: Gather all the flowers and foliage, and trim them to the desired size (I trimmed all of my materials to about ½ in [12 mm] lengths).

STEP 7: Starting at one end of the necklace, prepare the base by adding a fine layer of glue to a section of the template. For projects like this, composed of many petite ingredients, you may want to squeeze out a silver dollar–size pool of floral adhesive onto a paper plate or piece of cardboard. Dipping your materials into this reservoir of glue will allow you to add them to the prepared base quickly and easily. Dip each stem into the floral adhesive before pressing it onto the prepared base.

STEP 8: Work your way along the length of the piece, taking care to alternate colors and textures. Ingredients are added close together, sort of puzzle-pieced to create a tapestry of flowers. Press each addition down onto the base firmly, holding for 10 to 15 seconds to make sure each has adhered to the base. Play with depth, tucking darker or fuller items down at the base and allowing lighter or more transparent items to float above to create dimension in the arrangement.

PETAL PLAY NECKLACE

I'm a fashion addict and love to follow the global runway trends. I'm thrilled whenever I see the use of flowers on the fashion stage. Whether in large-scale floral installations used in set design or floral objets d'art on catwalks, or as accessories worn by the models, flowers and fashion are a natural pairing. One of my favorite applications, by makeup artist Val Garland for London Fashion Week 2017, inspired this playful design. In the Preen by Thornton Bregazzi show, whimsical dresses were paired with pressed petals and blooms, arranged directly on the skin—hugging the cheekbone, tracing the collarbone, and neatly arranged on the lips. In this design, the petals of hundreds of locally grown bachelor's buttons (which can be used fresh or dried) create a collar necklace ready for the runway.

MATERIALS:

- 10 bunches bachelor's button (*Centaurea cyanus*) in mixed colors
- Eyeliner pencil or brow liner pencil of your choice
- Elmer's glue or other nontoxic, skin-safe glue
- Paintbrush

STEP 1: Cut the blooms off of all the flowers and collect them in a bowl.

STEP 2: Grasp each flower, gathering and pinching the petals between your fingers, and trim them off into a container or bowl.

STEP 3: After all the petals are cut from their blooms, with your hands mix them in the bowl to combine the colors. Take your time with this step; it feels wonderful!

STEP 4: Using the eyeliner or brow liner pencil, trace the outline of the necklace onto your model. I used a brow liner color close to the shade of my model's skin tone.

STEP 5: Squeeze a generous amount of skin-safe glue into a bowl.

STEP 6: Working quickly, paint it onto the skin with your paintbrush, using the outline you drew as a guide.

STEP 7: Press the petals onto the glued necklace template, pressing firmly, adding to one small section at a time.

STEP 8: Perfect the placement by adding additional petals dipped in glue as needed.

STEP 9: To remove, simply wipe off with a moistened towel. Clean the skin with soap and water.

OVER-THE-EAR-EARRINGS

Sometimes the models I work with will inspire a design. It could be their personal style or coloring that sparks an idea or the use of certain materials. In this case, it was model Naomi's blunt bob and unpierced ears that informed the design of these over-the-ear earrings. I wanted to create dramatic, swingy, substantial earrings that would hang just below her bob. I created simple, adjustable loops with jewelry wire that I attached to slim, moon-shaped brass necklace blanks that simply slide over the helix of the ear. I chose light, feathery materials with a natural hanging shape in shades of pale pink, peach, and white to play up Naomi's hairstyle and creamy skin tone. For the blanks, I used 3½ by 1 in (9 by 2.5 cm) dapped brass bases from www.jansjewels.com.

MATERIALS:

- 20-gauge gold jewelry wire
- 2 crescent-shaped brass blanks with holes on either side
- Needle-nose jewelry pliers
- 1 or 2 stems coral hanging amaranthus
- 2 or 3 stems pink feather celosia (*Celosia spicata*)
- 2 or 3 stems pale pink dianthus
- 2 or 3 stems white salvia
- 1 or 2 stems immature pokeberry blooms (*Phytolacca americana*)
- 2 or 3 stems hosta buds and blooms (hyacinth or tuberose would also work well)
- 3 to 5 stems pale pink gomphrena
- 2 or 3 stems didiscus
- 1 or 2 stems pale pink astrantia
- 1 or 2 stems white ageratum
- Oasis floral adhesive

STEP 1: Measure two lengths of jewelry wire to 12 in (30 cm) and cut.

STEP 2: Feed one end of the wire through one end of the brass blank.

STEP 3: Twist it closed using the pliers. Repeat with the other end of the wire on the opposite side.

STEP 4: With both secured to the base, bring the two wires together, taking care to be sure they're even. Pull taut and twist the wires together to join them. This creates the loop that will allow the earring to be worn over the ear.

STEP 5: Trim all the flowers to usable lengths. I trimmed all the dangly materials—the hanging amaranthus, celosia, dianthus buds, salvia, and pokeberry blooms—to 1 to 3½ in (2.5 to 9 cm) lengths. Remove the stems from the hosta, gomphrena, and didiscus completely. Pull the dianthus petals from the calyx—these will be used individually.

STEP 6: Add a fine layer of the floral adhesive to the base, and wait 10 to 15 seconds to let it get tacky. Set a little bowl or scrap of cardboard by your work area and squeeze a small amount of glue onto it. Dip the end of each flower in the glue before adding it to the jewelry base.

STEP 7: The first layer of flowers to add to the base are the longest, most dangly materials—the hanging amaranth, celosia, and dianthus buds. Attach them securely to the base, allowing them to cascade down. Press and hold each element for 10 to 15 seconds to be sure it's adhered. The hanging materials will extend past the gluing platform, so you can add more floral layers along their entire length and/or over the top of the base.

STEP 8: Add the next floral layer—the dianthus petals, astrantia, salvia, and hosta buds and blooms. These add fullness and coverage.

STEP 9: Add the pokeberry blooms and white ageratum, floating them over the last floral layer, creating dimension and interest.

STEP 10: Add the front-facing flowers—the gomphrena, didiscus, and hosta buds—clustering them for effective groupings.

STEP 11: Inspect the earrings, making sure each side is complete, especially the sides that will frame the face.

STEP 12: Test the earrings on yourself or your model, adding or releasing twists in the wire to secure the loops over the ears and perfect the fit.

CHENILLE CHOKER

This design is inspired by one of my floral idols, Hitomi Gilliam. Before I saw Hitomi's creations, I had never really used chenille stems (more commonly known as pipe cleaners). The base of this choker consists of a slim, simple metal choker and a series of S-shaped chenille stem swirls. (I used the 17 in [43 cm] copper-coated steel choker from www.jansjewels.com; see "Resources," page 218.) The swirls hook onto the metal base and each other, allowing the freedom to create whatever shape you desire for your necklace platform.

The carnation petals "peek" out from under subsequent floral layers, adding their interesting color and providing body and dimension. I love how they recall the ruffled placket of a vintage tuxedo shirt.

MATERIALS:

- 25 to 30 chenille stems

- 1 slim metal choker necklace base

- 5 to 8 stems variegated carnation

- 3 to 5 stems cosmos blooms

- 3 to 5 stems blushing bride protea

- 5 to 8 stems pale pink spray carnation, Chabaud series 'La France'

- 3 to 5 stems hosta blooms

- 5 to 8 stems heuchera foliage

- 3 or 4 stems rose of Sharon blooms (*Hibiscus syriacus*)

- 3 to 5 stems Japanese anemone

- Oasis floral adhesive

- Dress form or mannequin form (optional)

STEP 1: Coil each chenille stem, beginning at one end of the stem and curling it into a tight, flat, disk-shaped coil.

STEP 2: Curl until you reach the midpoint of the stem, then starting at the other end, curl in the opposite direction, forming another equally sized disk. With the ends coiled in opposite directions, each stem will form an "S" shape.

STEP 3: Attach the curled chenille stems to the metal necklace base by twisting them twice at their central point to secure. Work your way around the base, adding multiple stems to add fullness to desired areas and linking stems to each other as well as to the base.

STEP 4: Prepare the flowers and foliage. Free the carnation petals from their calyxes and trim the cosmos, protea, spray carnation, and hosta blooms from their stems. Trim the heuchera foliage and rose of Sharon, but retain a bit of stem length. The stems will adhere to the necklace, locking the materials in place, but will also give them a little height, allowing them to float over the other materials.

STEP 5: Add a fine layer of the floral adhesive to the base, one section at a time, and wait 10 to 15 seconds to let it get tacky. Set a little bowl or scrap of cardboard by your work area and squeeze a small amount of glue onto it. Dip the end of each flower in the glue before adding it to the jewelry base.

STEP 6: Add the carnation petals, grouping them to add fullness and a lovely ruffled texture.

STEP 7: Add the flowers, starting with the pale pink spray carnations. Add multiple blooms to the upper left section to create an area of fullness.

STEP 8: Continue with the cosmos, protea, and rose of Sharon, repeating the placement pattern you began with, clustering them for fullness as desired.

STEP 9: Put the necklace onto the dress form. At this stage, all of the large, heavy flowers have been added, and the bulk of the base should be covered. Continue with the delicate hosta blooms and buds.

STEP 10: Next add the heuchera leaves, adding glue to their stems and nestling them into the floral landscape you've created. Tuck them into three spots, again repeating the placement pattern.

STEP 11: Finish with the Japanese anemone florets and buds.

The saying "Necessity is the mother of invention" perfectly describes how I came to make succulent jewelry. A few years ago I was asked to send a variety of floral jewelry pieces to California to be part of a photo shoot. The pieces would have to survive the journey from Michigan to California, arrive a few days ahead of the event, and then last four to five days. I knew I wouldn't be able to use fresh flowers, so I made the jewelry with succulents and long-lasting pods and berries. When I received the gorgeous photos from the shoot a few weeks later, I knew I was on to something good. In those first pieces, I incorporated dried materials as well, but as I experimented further and made more pieces, I found I was most attracted to jewelry made entirely of succulents in shades of green. Many, many hours of experimentation and testing later, I had crafted a style that I love.

As I began to share my succulent designs online, the excitement they generated prompted me to open an Etsy store, and I found myself making and shipping succulent corsages, cuffs, necklaces, crowns, rings, and earrings throughout the country. Media attention resulted in more orders than I was comfortable with, and early this year, after four years online, I decided to close the shop and stop staying up late making and packaging these beauties. I'd much rather share my love for them and teach people how to create their own. The pieces I share in this chapter are made with sedums, sempervivums, crassulas, and echeverias that I have tested extensively. I buy nearly all of my plants at Graye's, a local, family-owned greenhouse near my home that's been around for a hundred years. Their plants are strong, healthy, and well cared for—the perfect source for these little jewels. I encourage you to seek out your own local market, garden center, or greenhouse. I often buy large plants, keeping the tender ones indoors as houseplants, and planting the hardy ones in my garden so I can continue to cut from them year after year. The best part about succulent jewelry is that it's truly sustainable—the plants can be removed and potted after wear, and the jewelry bases can be either spiffed up and worn as minimalist jewelry or kept to be "planted" again.

When cutting the pieces I'll be using from the plants, I typically cut the larger succulents right below the leaf or floret but leave a bit of stem on the smaller ones. Note: *Sedum morganianum* can be delicate, and too much jostling can cause the leaves to fall off. To prevent this, I recommend carefully adding glue up into the body of the floret, in between the leaves, and along the length of the stem before adding them to the design.

SUCCULENT RING

Floral adhesive doesn't bond well to nonporous metal, so starting with a moss base layer gives the plants a sturdy platform to attach to. For my design I chose hardy hens and chicks (sempervivum or *Jovibarba heuffelii*); sedeveria 'Blue Elf', slightly smaller than the focal floret; Corsican stone-crop (*Sedum dasyphyllum* 'Major'); lamb's tail (*Sedum morganianum*); and string of pearls (*Senecio rowleyanus*).

MATERIALS:

• Variety of succulent
  cuttings, ranging from
  ¼ to 1 in (6 mm to 2.5 cm)

• Oasis floral adhesive

• 1 ring base

• Moss

STEP 1: Trim all the succulents from their stems. Add a fine layer of glue to the ring base and wait 10 to 15 seconds for the glue to get tacky.

STEP 2: Press fine threads of moss firmly onto the ring base.

STEP 3: Add another fine layer of glue on top of the moss.

STEP 4: Trim your largest, focal succulent flush, add a bit of glue to its underside, and press it onto the base, slightly off-center.

STEP 5: Add glue to another plant, nestle it next to the focal plant, and press to secure it into place.

STEP 6: Add a third floret with a bit of stem length to add a little height variation and a more interesting composition.

STEP 7: Finish and perfect your design by adding small flourishes of string of pearls.

CHUNKY CUFF

I've made hundreds of these eye-catching pieces over the years, and even though each one is slightly different, the diagonal design of the plants remains a constant. Because the bracelet base is bold and significant in size (I prefer a 4 In [10 cm] length), I like to balance the strength of it with a slim, diagonal, slightly more feminine arrangement of plants; this breaks up the visual weight of the hefty jewelry piece and creates an interesting marriage of strength and softness. I used the rosary vine to add interest to the focal area and the string of pearls to add the perfect tapered finish to the design's outer edges.

MATERIALS:

- Variety of succulent cuttings, ranging from ¼ to 2 in (12 mm to 5 cm)
- One 4 in (10 cm) adjustable brass cuff blank
- Oasis floral adhesive
- Dried sheet of sphagnum moss

STEP 1: Trim all the succulents from their stems.

STEP 2: Gently remove any dirt, spent leaves, or roots from the succulent florets.

STEP 3: Trace a diagonal line across the surface of the cuff with a fine layer of glue.

STEP 4: Select single threads of moss and press them firmly onto the glue line. Try pressing and rolling the base onto a piece of cardboard or sheet of waste paper to make sure the moss is firmly locked in place.

STEP 5: After the moss is securely attached, add another fine layer of glue on top of the moss.

STEP 6: Select the succulent florets you plan to use. Choose one special, slightly larger floret for the center of the piece and 2 slightly smaller florets of a different plant variety for either side. Add glue to the undersides of all 3 florets and wait 15 to 20 seconds to allow it to get tacky.

STEP 7: Press the central floret into the base and hold for 20 seconds. When this feels secure, add the 2 supporting florets, one on either side. Press each one down and hold for 20 seconds.

STEP 8: Start adding smaller florets to either side, adding glue to the underside of each before pressing it into place. Be sure to alternate plant varieties. Select plants by size, decreasing in size as you work your way across to the edges of the cuff. Alternate plant types and orientation to create a mosaic of elements that looks finished from all angles.

STEP 9: Complete the piece with delicate finishing elements such as string of pearl tendrils and rosary vine.

SUCCULENT EARRINGS

These playful, swingy earrings are fun to wear, quick to make, and require just a tiny handful of petite plants. The brass drops I've used are pear-shaped, but bases are available in myriad widths, lengths, and shapes. I used 14K gold wires. Experiment with different styles, and wear them for an unexpected flash of green. I chose lamb's tail (*Sedum morganianum*), sedeveria 'Blue Elf', and string of pearls (*Senecio rowleyanus*)—three trailing tendrils on each earring and a little cluster of pearls above the sedums.

MATERIALS:

- Succulent cuttings, ranging from ½ to 1 in (12 mm to 2.5 cm)
- Oasis floral adhesive
- 1 pair 1½ by 1 in (4 by 2.5 cm) brass drops fitted with ear wire
- Dried sheet of sphagnum moss

STEP 1: Trim all the succulents from their stems.

STEP 2: Gently remove any dirt, spent leaves, or roots from the succulent florets.

STEP 3: Add a fine layer of floral glue to the surface of both brass drops.

STEP 4: Select single threads of moss and press them firmly onto the glued drops. After the moss is firmly attached, add another fine layer of glue on top of the moss.

STEP 5: Add glue to the undersides of all the florets, and wait 15 to 20 seconds to allow it to get tacky. Press the central floret into the base and hold for 20 seconds. When this feels secure, add the 2 supporting florets to each base. Arrange them above the central floret, next to each other, turning them until the leaves interlock for added security. With each addition, press down and hold for 20 seconds.

STEP 6: Finish the piece by adding delicate, trailing string of pearl tendrils.

BOW TIE

It's a shame that men don't have more fun with floral fashion. Typically, men wear flowers only a handful of times in their lives—likely in the form of a simple boutonniere—at weddings, school dances, or perhaps a special black-tie affair. In all my years of designing weddings, I had only a few grooms who took interest in the flowers they were asked to wear. My favorite, Eli, was very interested in flowers and knew exactly what he wanted for his wedding: a botanical bow tie. I had so much fun making this for him, and it was a nice change to see a man engaged in the floral aspect of his wedding.

MATERIALS:

- 1 special larger succulent for the central "knot" section
- Variety of tiny succulent cuttings, ranging from ⅛ to 1 in (4 mm to 2.5 cm)
- Oasis floral adhesive
- 1 bow-tie base

STEP 1: Trim all the succulents, including the larger one, from their stems.

STEP 2: Gently remove any dirt, spent leaves, or roots.

STEP 3: Add glue to the central "knot" section of the bow-tie base. Add a fine layer of glue to the back of the larger succulent. Wait 10 to 15 seconds to allow the glue on the base and the plant to get tacky, then press the succulent onto the center of the tie base and hold firmly for 10 to 15 seconds to ensure it's well bonded.

STEP 4: Add a fine layer of glue to one half of the bow-tie base and wait 10 to 15 seconds to let it get tacky.

STEP 5: Starting at the inner edge of the base, add petite succulents, placing them very close together and alternating varieties. Add a bit of glue to each underside before placing it on the base. Gently but firmly press each plant to the base and hold for a few seconds to ensure it adheres.

STEP 6: Continue to add plants, gradually working your way to the outer edge of the tie. Alternate type and orientation of the plants to create a mosaic of elements that looks beautiful from all angles.

STEP 7: When you've completed the first side of the tie, fill in the other side of the tie in the same fashion as the first.

STEP 8: Complete the piece by tucking delicate elements like the string of pearls into tiny empty spaces that would otherwise be difficult to fill.

COLLAR NECKLACE

I love big, dramatic statement necklaces. When I need to dress up for a social occasion, I often pair a simple dress or jumpsuit with a chunky collar necklace. The weightiness of the jewelry grounds and emboldens me a bit. And it sparks conversation, directing attention away from my social unease and toward a topic I love: fashion. The unexpected and unusual quality of this succulent collar necklace could easily carry conversation through the entire length of a party, making it the perfect accessory for those who are small talk–challenged like me. I used lamb's tail (*Sedum morganianum*), sedeveria 'Blue Elf', and hardy hens and chicks (sempervivum or *Jovibarba heuffelii*). I used around fifty 1½ to 2 in (4 to 5 cm) sedeveria and sempervivum and around forty ½ to 1 in (12 mm to 2.5 cm) sedum, sempervivum, and sedeveria plants.

MATERIALS:

- Variety of succulent cuttings, ranging from ½ to 3 in (12 mm to 7.5 cm)

- Oasis floral adhesive

- ¾ in (2 cm) adjustable brass collar necklace base

- 2 small air plants (*Tillandsia*)

- 10 to 15 strands string of pearls (*Senecio rowleyanus*)

STEP 1: Trim all the succulents from their stems.

STEP 2: Gently remove any dirt, spent leaves, or roots.

STEP 3: Work in sections of a few inches at a time. Add a fine layer of glue to the necklace base. Starting at one end, add the smallest succulents, placing them very close together and alternating varieties.

STEP 4: Add a bit of glue to each plant's underside before placing it on the base. Gently but firmly press each plant and hold to the base for 10 to 15 seconds to ensure it adheres.

STEP 5: Continue to add plants, including small sections of the air plants, gradually working up to larger and larger florets. Alternate type and orientation to create a mosaic of elements that looks beautiful from all angles.

STEP 6: When you reach the center, spend a little more time focusing on the sides of the design—facing some plants up toward the top of the piece, and others downward—puzzle piecing them together to create a full, finished focal area and taking care to cover every bit of the brass base.

STEP 7: Work your way down the length of the other side of the necklace, selecting plants to gradually diminish in size.

STEP 8: Complete the piece by adding delicate finishing elements such as string of pearl tendrils. Use them to float over larger plants, or to tuck into tiny empty spaces that would otherwise be difficult to fill.

As a self-appointed corsage ambassador, I feel compelled to share my love for the art of corsage making widely. Corsages have a huge public relations problem. Most florists I talk to are beyond weary of the tradition, and for good reason. They argue that corsages look dated, trite, or garish. Beyond the aesthetic issues, many just plain hate the drudgery of making them. People often recount their training in this work—they were taught to wire all the botanical components (commonly spray roses, stiff greenery, and a filler flower like baby's breath) and combine them with a mass of looped ribbon. This collection of materials was then typically strapped to an inexpensive elastic wristlet, or some sort of tacky, sparkly rhinestone-encrusted corsage bracelet. I was trained this way. I've made more than a thousand corsages for others over the years, and when I opened my own studio I was determined that my offerings would be different. I wanted to see streamlined, sophisticated, simple, flower-forward corsages that exemplify the moment. I wanted to combine my love of jewelry design and flowers by pairing interesting, unexpected botanicals with sleek jewelry bases instead of stretchy elastic. In these pages I outline my preferred ways of making corsages—techniques that offer design ease, wearability, and a contemporary feel. I hope they inspire new designers to fall in love with corsages—and jaded florists to give them another try.

3 / FASHION-FORWARD CORSAGES

FLORAL BANGLE

My dear friend Holly Chapple, florist extraordinaire, opened my eyes to this design years ago. We were hanging out at her floral conference, sitting at a table full of floral detritus—abandoned florets, stray greenery and herbs, and spent stem wrap tape rolls. She showed me how to make a bangle using the tape roll by quickly whipping up the sweetest little floral bracelet using the ingredients on the table. This design is essentially a miniature wreath, made by laying little floral bundles onto the base (in Holly's case, a spent tape roll that she had snipped open) one by one, each bundle covering the stems of the last, until the circle is complete. This a fun-to-make, fun-to-wear, unexpected, playful alternative to the standard corsage.

MATERIALS:

- 2 or 3 stems white spray chrysanthemum (mum)
- 1 stem green antique hydrangea
- 2 or 3 stems Japanese spray rose 'Eclair'
- 2 or 3 stems white agapanthus
- Stem wrap tape

- 1 stem blooming feather acacia
- 1 calocephalus plant (herbs, bleached fern, or feather acacia would also work well)
- 1 bangle bracelet (the snipped inner ring from a spent stem wrap tape roll also works well)

- Oasis 28-gauge bullion wire, gold
- 1 stem white hyacinth
- Oasis floral adhesive

NOTE: Some of the materials have soft stems, so it's essential to tape them together first—this ensures that the wire used to bind them to the bracelet base won't cut into their stems, causing breakage.

STEP 1: Prepare all your bundles before assembling. Cut the mums, hydrangea florets, Japanese spray roses, and agapanthus florets to a stem length of 1 to 2 in (2.5 to 5 cm). Bundle the mums, hydrangea, and roses in 2 or 3 stem bunches and bind them together with the stem wrap tape. Gather the dainty agapanthus florets in 8 to 10 stem bunches and bind with tape. Trim the sturdy acacia and calocephalus stems to your desired length; no need to tape these.

STEP 2: Choose a place on the bangle and firmly wrap it with a little piece of the stem wrap tape; this is where you'll start attaching florets. Roll out and cut a length of the bullion wire, about 12 in (30.5 cm) long; for this piece, it's much easier to work with when it's not attached to the roll. Begin by attaching the wire to the taped spot on the bangle: press one end of the wire to the taped area, and wrap the wire over itself to secure it to the taped portion of the bangle.

STEP 3: Start adding materials: Press a floral bundle against the bracelet, pull the wire taut, and wrap it around the taped portion of the bundle a few times. Continue to add bundles, alternating varieties and the direction the blooms are facing, working your way around the base. With each addition, pull the wire downward, keeping it taut, and wrap it around the taped portion of the bundle a few times to secure it to the bangle base.

STEP 4: Once you have added all the bundles, trim and secure any remaining wire to the bangle base. Now comes the fun part—add delicate hyacinth florets to the piece using floral adhesive. Cut the blooms from their stems, dip them in the floral glue, and find secure spaces within the tight network of wired stems you just created to tuck them into. Cluster some of these delicate flowers together for interest and impact.

STEP 5: Add little bits of the calocephalus plant, acacia, or agapanthus buds to the piece to complete it and add movement.

STEP 6: To prevent flattening on one side, take care to store this piece in a box lined with plenty of loose shredded paper.

PETITE RIBBON CORSAGE

I love the simplicity and ease of this corsage style. I've seen many ribbon corsages in my day, but I've been underwhelmed with the techniques used to make them. My method is incredibly simple and creates a very reliable and sound platform for adding flowers. A yard of ribbon is long enough to tie a nice bow with streamers below the wrist. I create platforms out of faux leather that I glue to my ribbon before adding flowers. These little bases can be made ahead of time, and they are both quick and easy to make and very economical. The resulting corsages are comfortable, structurally sound, and fun to make and wear. I use raw silk ribbon from May Arts.

MATERIALS:

- 3 by 1 in (7.5 by 2.5 cm) oval cardboard or paper template
- Faux leather
- Hot glue (optional)
- Oasis floral adhesive
- 1 yd (91 cm) soft ribbon
- 1 stem pink garden spray rose
- 1 stem ranunculus
- 1 stem Japanese spray rose 'Eclair'
- 1 stem nerine lily
- 1 stem blooming feather acacia

STEP 1: Use the cardboard template to cut an oval shape out of the faux leather. This platform provides a reliable base for all the floral materials.

STEP 2: Glue the oval platform onto the midpoint of the ribbon, using hot glue or floral adhesive. Press the platform firmly onto the ribbon and smooth it down.

STEP 3: Add a fine layer of floral glue to the corsage platform. Cut the pink garden spray rose blossom (the largest bloom) flush, add glue to its base, and place it on the platform, slightly off-center. Press down and hold it firmly for 10 to 15 seconds.

STEP 4: Cut the ranunculus flush, remove the sepals, add glue to its base, and press it next to the rose.

STEP 5: With the central blooms attached, move on to the secondary blooms. Squeeze a small amount of floral adhesive into a small bowl. Cut individual Japanese spray rose blooms off their main stem, dip them into the glue reservoir, and tuck them in next to the heavier central flowers, pressing each down to ensure good attachment to the platform.

STEP 6: Now add the delicate nerine. Cut the blooms from their stem, dip them into the glue, and find a nice spot to tuck them in next to the other flowers.

STEP 7: Finish with the acacia florets. Dip their stems in glue and add them to the piece, allowing them to cascade off the platform, adding interest and movement.

STEP 8: Analyze the piece from all sides to make sure the entire platform is covered. Add elements to perfect the shape and look of the piece and fill any gaps.

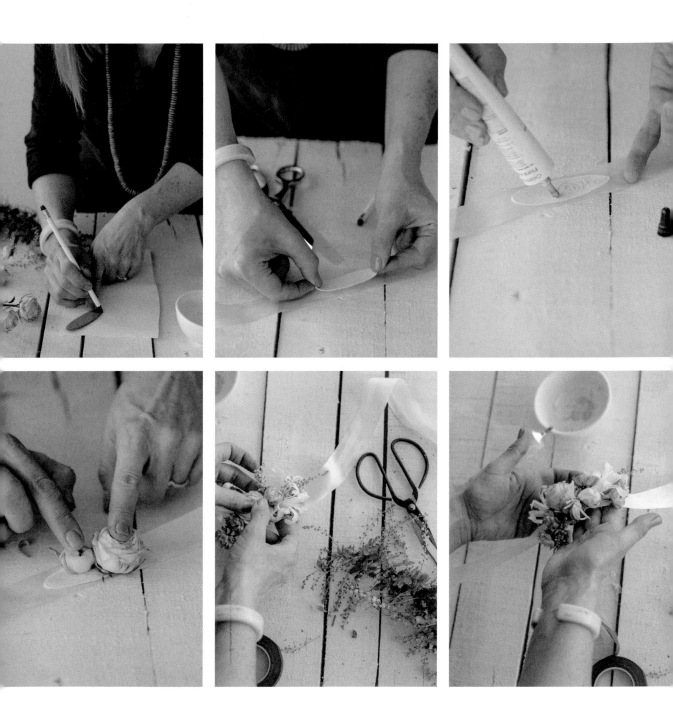

SHOULDER CORSAGE

When you think of shoulder corsages, you may picture dated, bulky clusters of flowers finished with a mass of stiff ribbon. This style still prevails, but there is another way. When I began making floral jewelry and started experimenting with faux leather, it clicked that I could create streamlined, updated, light-as-a-feather shoulder corsages using this fabric as the base. The faux leather is sturdy enough to hold the weight of flowers but soft and supple enough to hug the body's contours. Instead of the time-consuming and bulky traditional wiring, here the floral material is simply glued to the faux leather base. The corsages can be attached to delicate gauzy fabrics using corsage magnets or to thicker fabrics with corsage pins.

MATERIALS:

- Faux leather fabric
- 1 or 2 stems Japanese lisianthus (*Eustoma grandiflorum*)
- Oasis floral adhesive
- 1 stem blooming feather acacia
- 1 stem spray rose 'Earth'
- 1 stem Japanese spray rose 'Eclair'
- 1 stem agapanthus
- 2 or 3 stems hellebore
- Corsage pins or corsage magnets

NOTE: Hellebore become sturdy and reliable for use in wearable work only after they have gone to seed.

STEP 1: Sketch and cut a shape out of the faux leather to make the corsage base.

STEP 2: Cut the lisianthus from its stem and cut the blossom in half to reduce its large size and high profile. Used on its side, its ruffles adds texture to the design.

STEP 3: Add glue to the corsage base and squeeze a small amount into a bowl. Take 3 lisianthus petals and dip them, front and back, into the glue. Press the petals onto the base and hold firmly for 10 to 15 seconds.

STEP 4: Dip the acacia into your glue reservoir and add it to the base, letting it cascade off the side. Place the acacia next to the 3 lisianthus petals.

STEP 5: Cut the 'Earth' roses from their stems, dip them in the glue, and press them onto the base.

STEP 6: Cut the Japanese spray roses flush. Dip them in the glue and find a nice spot to cluster a few of them. Leave a little length on one and float it above the others to create depth and interest. Cluster a few more of the these around the 'Earth' roses.

STEP 7: Cut a few agapanthus florets and tuck them in to cover any remaining base and add texture.

STEP 8: Cut a few more agapanthus blooms with their stems. Dip their stem tips into the glue and stand them up, allowing them to float over the other elements in the design.

STEP 9: Cut the hellebore stem, retaining a little stem length. Apply glue and find a nice focal point for these special blooms.

STEP 10: Check the perimeter for unfinished areas and add small details throughout to complete the piece.

STEP 11: To attach, first position the corsage on the garment. Press the corsage to the fabric and lift both away from the wearer to protect the skin from the corsage pins. Find a nice spot between blooms in the top of the piece and, angling the corsage pin downward, guide the tip of the pin into the leather base of the corsage and through the garment, pushing the pin down ¼ to ½ in (6 to 12 mm) or so, then start angling the pin upward and guide its point back through the garment and the corsage base. Make sure that the point rests fully on the surface of the corsage, not underneath the corsage next to the wearer's skin. Insert another pin in the same way on the opposite side of the piece, approaching from the top and orienting the pin downward to secure the corsage in place. If you plan to use corsage magnets, attach them to the faux leather base using floral adhesive—one on either side—before adding flowers.

CUFF CORSAGE

This bold cuff is my most asked about corsage project. I've designed these special pieces to be worn by bridesmaids in place of carrying the traditional bouquet, for fashion-forward prom-goers, and as accessories for various dressy celebrations. I love that a generous amount of floral materials can be artfully displayed on the ample 4 in (10 cm) bracelet base, and I'm pleased with how easily this project comes together. You can create movement in these designs by choosing a variety of materials — larger, low-profile blooms to build the base layer, and lighter, floaty materials to "dance" above the heavier ones.

MATERIALS:

- 3 by 1 in (7.5 by 2.5 cm) oval cardboard or paper template
- Faux leather fabric
- Oasis floral adhesive
- 4 in (10 cm) brass cuff bracelet base
- 1 stem white ranunculus
- 1 stem white strawflower
- 1 stem white spray mum
- 1 stem Japanese spray rose 'Eclair'
- 1 stem white hyacinth
- 1 stem white agapanthus
- 1 stem blooming feather acacia

STEP 1: Using an oval template, trace a small oval on the faux leather and cut it out.

STEP 2: Add a fine layer of glue and place it diagonally on the bracelet base; this will be your gluing platform.

STEP 3: Cut the ranunculus flush, removing any damaged petals and the sepals. Add a little glue to the underside of the flower and also to the corsage base. Place the ranunculus on the top third of the base and hold it for 10 to 15 seconds until it adheres.

STEP 4: Cut the strawflower flush, add glue to the base of the flower, and nestle it in next to the ranunculus, pressing to attach.

STEP 5: Cut the mums, leaving a range of stem lengths, 1 to 1½ in (2.5 to 4 cm). Squeeze a small amount of glue into a little bowl and keep it close. Dip the shortest mum stem in the glue reservoir and nestle it underneath the flowers on the base. Repeat with a mum with the next longest stem. Place a third mum on the opposite side of the piece. Add a slightly smaller-headed and longer-stemmed mum next to this one to complement it.

STEP 6: Cut a large Japanese spray rose bloom flush and add glue to its base. Nestle a flower next to the mums, pressing and holding for 10 to 15 seconds until it adheres. Cut more roses, keeping a little bit of the stem length to be able to float them above the other flowers, and glue them in throughout the piece.

STEP 7: Cut off individual hyacinth florets, add glue to the base of each bloom, and tuck them into the little crevices between the larger blooms.

STEP 8: Cut buds of agapanthus from their main stem, leaving the long individual stem on each. Add glue to the ends of the stems and tuck them into the design so they float over the other ingredients, creating interest and movement.

STEP 9: Finish with the delicate acacia blooms. Lift up the focal flowers and tuck the acacia in underneath to give that area more texture and color. Choose another spot on the opposite side of the piece, and repeat with a smaller stem of acacia.

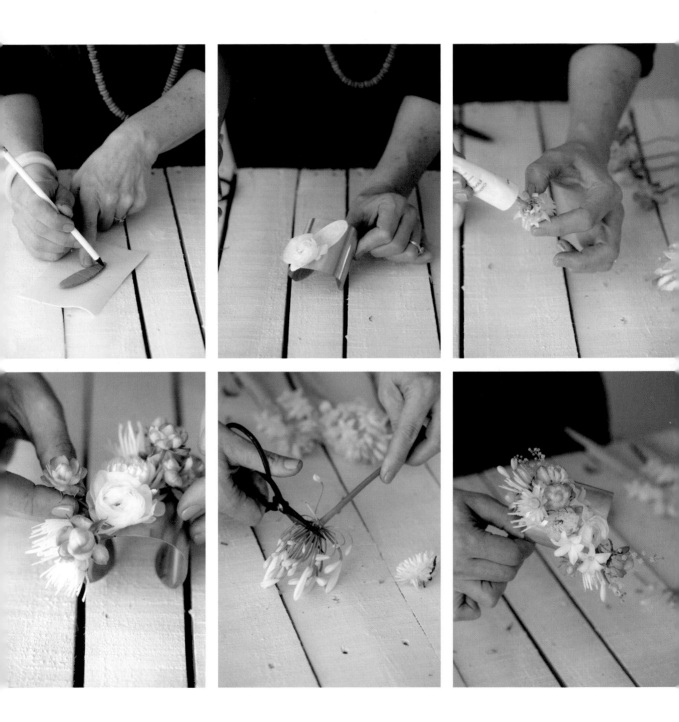

ARTFUL WIRED CUFF

This stylish corsage is currently my favorite to make. Over the last several years, I've enjoyed sharing my cuff corsage techniques. Students have overwhelmingly embraced the look of these sleek floral bracelets, and they've found that using floral adhesive to attach the floral components is efficient and secure. However, some say that while they love the look of these pieces, they miss the control and extra stability that traditional wiring offers. I'm pleased to share a way to marry the sleek look of a cuff corsage with the security and control of wiring. I used a simple brass cuff with a center (swedge) hole for this project, but any sturdy cuff-style bracelet with at least one hole in its surface will work well.

MATERIALS:

- 24-gauge floral wire
- 1 or 2 stems spray rose 'Earth'
- 2 or 3 stems peach lisianthus
- 1 or 2 stems variegated carnation, petals removed
- 1 or 2 stems rose sumac

- 5 to 7 stems raspberry scabiosa
- Stem wrap tape
- One ¾ in (2 cm) self-adhesive felt pad
- 1 chenille stem
- One 3 in (7.5 cm) brass cuff with a center (swedge) hole

- UGlu tabs or sturdy double-stick tape
- Oasis floral adhesive (optional)

STEP 1: Wire the spray roses and lisianthus using the piercing technique; the carnation petals and rose sumac using the cranking technique; and the scabiosa using the insertion technique. (For more on this, see "Wiring Techniques" on page 28.)

STEP 2: To create the attachment platform for the corsage, carefully pierce two holes through the felt pad. Bend the chenille stem into a slender "U" shape and feed it through the holes so the free ends of the chenille stem emerge on the adhesive side of the felt pad.

STEP 3: Peel off the felt pad's paper backing and feed the ends of the chenille stem through the hole in the corsage base. Pull to snug up the chenille stem and twist the ends to secure it. This will be the attachment point for the wired component of the corsage.

STEP 4: Add UGlu tabs to the corsage base on either side of the central attachment point. This makes the piece more secure.

STEP 5: To create the wired floral component of the corsage, start with the most tapered element—the rose sumac. Add a carnation petal bundle, placing it below the sumac so its ruffled petals cover the taped portion of the sumac stem. Use stem wrap tape to secure.

STEP 6: Add the next-largest component—a spray rose—again staggering the placement so the head of the flower covers the stem end of the one previous, and lock into place with stem wrap tape.

STEP 7: Add more blooms, locking each in place with stem wrap tape, using increasingly larger sizes until you reach the center of the piece. As you place them, gently bend the wire to orient the stems slightly left and slightly right so the design is finished looking from all sides.

STEP 8: Now choose increasingly smaller components until you reach the end of the piece. You can choose how long to make the wired piece—perhaps cascading off the cuff a few inches on either side.

STEP 9: When you reach the end of the piece, choose a final stem to finish the design and conceal your mechanics. Bend the wire at the base of the bloom completely to meet the wired stem. Tuck it in tightly to finish the design.

STEP 10: If the design has gaps, or tape is visible from the sides of the piece, use floral adhesive to easily add finishing details where needed.

The "floral tattoo" idea was sparked when I happened upon an instructional video by the gifted floral artist Shawn Michael Foley. He shared how to attach petite floral groupings directly to the skin. They were made to accompany the incredible full-body wearable artworks that make up his Human Form Project.

When I tried my hand at designing floral tattoos, I needed a base material that would stick to the skin without harming it, flex but stay put with movement, and be waterproof and impermeable to the floral glue I planned to use. A browse through my local pharmacy provided the perfect solution—waterproof kinesiology tape! This tape is created to be worn during sports activities, so it is sweat-proof, waterproof, flexible yet strong, and comfortable against the skin.

These floral tattoos can be petite or grand and worn anywhere on the body. They are fun and easy to make—requiring only tape, glue, and flowers. They also make a fantastic group activity for a bridal shower, birthday, or floral workshop.

Although the mechanics are simple, a lot of thought goes into creating these little floral landscapes. I like mine to be intricately detailed and full of depth and dimension.

In this chapter, I share a variety of ideas—small to large, simple to complex—to give you insight into my steps and hopefully spark your own new ideas. I also share some bonus tattoo variations, all made with the same skills and supplies, to show some of the endless possibilities and adaptability of this concept. I encourage you to experiment with this idea and see where it takes you!

For all of these designs, it's important to remember to clean the skin with rubbing alcohol or other astringent before placing the tattoo tape. The tape will not stick well if natural oils and/or lotion are left on the skin.

CHAMOMILE FOUR-FINGER RINGS

I adore chamomile—its distinctive uplifting scent and the cheeriness of the blooms always puts an instant smile on my face. I can't resist buying huge armfuls when it's in season, and I think it looks best en masse. When it's in my studio, I keep a little sprig in my shirt pocket or behind my ear so I can take little sniffs all day. These four-finger ring tattoos would allow the wearer to do the same—aromatherapy accessories, anyone?

I used 3M brand narrow waterproof tape without a paper backing to make these, so they had to be made directly on the wearer. A sunshine-yellow dress and sprinkle of single blooms (attached to the delicate facial skin with eyelash adhesive) add to the playful vibe of this design.

MATERIALS:

- Rubbing alcohol or other astringent
- 3M Nexcare "absolute waterproof" tape (Band-Aids also work well)
- Oasis floral adhesive
- 10 stems chamomile
- Eyelash adhesive (optional)

STEP 1: Cleanse the skin with the astringent and allow to dry.

STEP 2: Apply the tape to the fingers by tearing appropriate lengths and creating a ring around each of the fingers on both hands.

STEP 3: Working on one finger at a time, add a fine layer of floral adhesive to the tape ring and wait 10 to 15 seconds to allow it to get tacky.

STEP 4: Cut the chamomile blooms from their stems and gather them in a little bowl or hold them gently in your hand. Add a little dot of glue to each bloom before adding it to the ring base. Press each bloom down firmly and hold for 5 to 10 seconds.

STEP 5: Continue to add blooms, working your way around each finger, adding blooms in layers to ensure full coverage.

STEP 6: Add tiny blooms to the face if desired, using eyelash adhesive instead of floral adhesive.

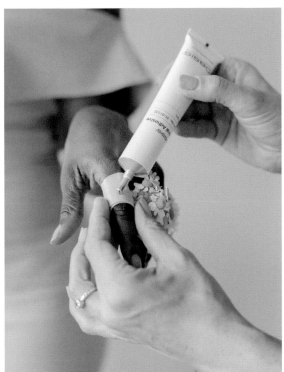

TATTOO CORSAGE

These tattoos can really be worn anywhere on the body, but I chose to show them on the wrists because I love the idea of this technique replacing (or at least challenging) the traditional wrist corsage. I would love to see those stiff, unimaginative relics laid to rest for good. Tattoo corsages celebrate the tradition of corsages while at the same time revolutionizing it. A tattoo corsage can be a DIY project made for a school dance or event, or it can be an offering at flower shops or studios. You can make it on kinesiology tape with a paper backing, or assemble it directly on the wearer. I imagine people coming into flower shops and getting "tattooed" before an event in the same way as they go to a hairstylist or makeup artist.

MATERIALS:

- Spartan brand waterproof kinesiology tape with a paper backing
- 2 or 3 stems orange butterfly snapdragon
- 3 to 5 stems *Scabiosa morgana* 'Yellow Pincushion'
- 1 or 2 stems coral hanging amaranthus
- 1 or 2 stems immature currant tomatoes
- 1 or 2 stems coral feather celosia (*Celosia spicata*)

- 5 to 7 stems zinnia 'Queen Lime'
- 3 to 5 stems zinnia 'Zinderella Peach'
- 2 or 3 stems orange strawflower
- 1 or 2 stems peach cockscomb celosia (*Celosia cristata*) or brain celosia
- 1 or 2 stems pale pink feather celosia (*Celosia spicata*)
- 1 or 2 stems immature dill blooms

- 1 stem immature bittersweet berries
- 1 stem miniature scented geranium
- Oasis floral adhesive
- Rubbing alcohol or other astringent

STEP 1: Measure the kinesiology tape to the desired length.

STEP 2: Sketch out the shape you'd like for the tattoo before cutting. Giving the pieces curves allows the body contours to show beneath the design. To create mirror-image tattoos as I did, sketch two mirror-image "S" designs on the tape.

STEP 3: Trim all the flowers to the desired length. Heavier or larger materials are typically cut flush so they can attach securely to the base. Cut the scabiosa, snapdragon, larger zinnia, and straw-flower flush, but keep a little length on the celosia and hanging amaranthus to make the most of their delicate, cascading quality, and on the dill florets, a few of the smaller zinnias, and the currant tomatoes so they can float over some of the heavier materials.

STEP 4: Add a fine layer of floral adhesive to the entire length of the tattoo. Squeeze out more adhesive—about a quarter-size pool at a time—into a little bowl or scrap of cardboard. As you add materials, dip each one into the glue before adding it to the tattoo base. Starting at one end of the piece, begin adding the daintiest materials, alternating varieties and placing them closely together. Choose from the smallest bits, or deconstruct the materials to create small bits to work with.

STEP 5: Continue adding materials, gradually working up to larger blooms and florets. Alternate type and orientation to create a mosaic of elements that looks beautiful from all angles.

STEP 6: When you reach the middle section, focus on the edges so the tape doesn't show. The largest blooms can be added here, as it's the fullest point of the tattoo. Nestle the flowers together, almost like puzzle pieces, for support and coverage and to create an interesting, textured design.

STEP 7: Work your way down the length of the base, selecting smaller and smaller flowers and bits as you go.

STEP 8: Complete the piece by "floating" top layer ingredients and delicate finishing elements.

STEP 9: Before placing the tattoos, cleanse the skin with astringent and allow it to dry.

BATEAU TATTOO

"Bateau" is a fashion term used to describe a neckline that runs horizontally across the shoulders, often tracing, or falling just below, the collarbone; this style is also called a "boat neck." When my friend (and gorgeous model) LaPorcshia showed up at my recent tattoo party in an adorable puffed-sleeve, off-the-shoulder bateau top, I knew I wanted to tattoo her collarbone to highlight this lovely part of the body. I created a partner tattoo to be worn with this piece, placed on the wrist on the opposite side of the body (see "Tattoo Corsage," page 127, for inspiration and instruction). I love how the pair draws the eye across the body, from the crest of the shoulder to the tip of the hand.

MATERIALS:

- Kinesiology tape
- Rubbing alcohol or other astringent
- 3 or 4 stems zinnia 'Queen Lime', for the buds
- 1 or 2 stems didiscus, for the buds
- 1 stem beautyberry (*Callicarpa*)
- 1 stem cockscomb celosia (*Celosia cristata*)
- 1 stem feather celosia (*Celosia spicata*)

- 1 or 2 stems gomphrena
- 3 to 5 stems scabiosa 'Black Knight'
- 1 stem hyacinth bean
- 1 stem red hanging amaranthus
- 5 to 7 stems 'Sugar Plum' and 'Sugar Berry' heuchera foliage
- Oasis floral adhesive

STEP 1: Measure the kinesiology tape to the desired length. Sketch out the shape you'd like for the tattoo, then cut.

STEP 2: Clean the skin area you plan to tattoo with astringent to remove natural oils and/or lotion from the surface of the skin.

STEP 3: Place the tattoo base on the skin.

STEP 4: Trim all the flowers to the desired length. Cut all the flowers flush except the hyacinth bean, hanging amaranthus, and heuchera foliage. Retain the stem length of the amaranthus to allow it to hang naturally. The stems of the heuchera leaves and hyacinth will float them over other heavier materials.

STEP 5: Add a fine layer of floral adhesive to the entire length of the tattoo. Squeeze out more adhesive—about a quarter-size pool at a time—into a little bowl or scrap of cardboard. As you add materials, dip each one into the glue before adding it to the tattoo base.

STEP 6: Working with the darkest materials first, dip each flower in the floral adhesive before pressing it onto the tattoo base.

STEP 7: Create a full-coverage base layer with the deep-toned scabiosa, cockscomb celosia, and gomphrena. Add the largest blooms to the center of the piece, and work your way down either side of the piece, tracing the line of the tape base, alternating varieties and selecting progressively smaller flowers and botanical bits.

STEP 8: Add the top layer. Try floating interesting finishing bits by gluing their stems and nestling them into the floral landscape below. This technique allows you to obscure the base a bit, play with color distribution, and create wonderful depth and dimension.

WRAPAROUND TATTOO

This is the design that began my exploration into floral tattoos. Because of the size of this piece, it's best made (or at least finished) on the model. If this isn't possible, I recommend using kinesiology tape with a paper backing and making a series of tattoos—one for the crown, one that spans the area between the cheekbone and base of the neck, a few short lengths to cup the shoulder, and one to span the length of the arm. On this large tattoo, it's helpful to work with one flower type at a time, adding each type throughout the length of the piece. (For insight into specific floral placement and color layering, see "Design Process," page 22, in "Tools and Techniques.")

MATERIALS:

- Rubbing alcohol or other astringent
- Waterproof kinesiology tape, cut to desired lengths
- 25 to 30 stems scabiosa 'Black Knight'
- 5 to 7 stems blushing bride protea
- 20 to 25 stems white zinnia
- 5 to 7 stems garden chrysanthemum 'Staviski Pink'
- 5 to 7 stems garden chrysanthemum 'Belgian Carpino Purple'
- 3 to 5 stems white snowberry (*Symphoricarpos*)
- 5 to 7 stems *Pieris japonica*
- 5 to 7 stems star of Bethlehem (*Ornithogalum dubium*)
- 15 to 20 stems white carnation, Chabaud series 'Jeanne Dionis'
- 15 to 20 stems 'Sugar Plum' heuchera foliage
- 5 to 7 stems *Astrantia major* 'Burgundy Manor'
- 1 stem white squill (*Urginea maritima*) for the florets
- 1 or 2 stems sweet pea for 7 to 10 tendrils
- Oasis floral adhesive

STEP 1: Cleanse the skin with astringent and allow to dry.

STEP 2: Using a series of manageable lengths, create the base of the tattoo by firmly pressing the tape pieces to the skin. Trace a continuous line from the center of the forehead, just under the hairline, around the side of the face, across the back of the neck, and down the entire length of the arm to the fingertip.

STEP 3: Add multiple short lengths of tape to cup the shoulder—the design will be fullest here.

STEP 4: Trim all the flowers to the desired length. Cut the scabiosa, blushing bride protea, zinnias, several of the mums, and snowberry flush. Retain some stem length of 1 in (2.5 cm) or so on the pieris, carnation, heuchera, and several of the smaller mum blooms to float over other deeper materials.

STEP 5: Add a fine film of adhesive to the tattoo base, spaced every few inches, preparing spots for your first floral type. Squeeze out more adhesive—about a quarter-size pool at a time—into a little bowl or scrap of cardboard. As you add materials, dip each one into this glue reservoir before adding it to the base.

STEP 6: Begin with the dark scabiosa. Dip each scabiosa bloom into your glue reservoir, then press against the glue spots on the tape. Hold each for 10 to 15 seconds to make sure the flower adheres.

STEP 7: Add the protea throughout, clustering blooms together to create areas of fullness. Follow with the zinnias, mums, snowberry, and pieris, one type at a time. These base layer elements should mostly cover the tape.

STEP 8: Add the rest of the materials, floating them above the base landscape: the carnation, astrantia, ornithogalum, heuchera foliage, and the remaining mums with slightly longer stems, floating these over the base layer.

STEP 9: Add the delicate finishing materials: tiny buds, white squill florets, and the sweet pea tendrils.

BONUS TATTOO VARIATIONS:

Floral tattoos can be worn in so many ways, and the following variations showcase a variety of tattoos I've made in the past. A few simple tweaks to an existing concept can make it work for a different part of the body.

For example, to make the Shoe Tattoo below, I followed the same steps as the Tattoo Corsage (page 127) but placed the arrangement on a shoe. I hope these variations inspire you to experiment with your own floral tattoos—a single design can offer endless possibilities!

The practice of wearing flowers in the hair is centuries old—flower crowns have been worn to celebrate weddings, festivals, and religious ceremonies. In recent years, the flower crown experienced a renaissance of sorts, and after reaching a coolness crescendo, unfortunately it became a bit of a cliché. But I firmly believe there is still a time and place for a flower crown. I often make flower crowns for friends' birthdays, graduations, and retirements—really, any cause for celebration. I love how special people feel upon receiving a crown, and how it instantly increases the celebratory vibe of a gathering. To make a special, one-of-a-kind crown, choose unexpected flowers, or create a piece that sits on the head in an unexpected way—such as the arc-shaped Demi-Crown or the petite Floral Fascinator. I encourage you to take inspiration from the projects in the upcoming pages and create a reason to "crown" yourself, and your loved ones, as often as possible.

SIMPLEST FLOWER CROWN

This crown, made with a single flower type, is the perfect project to start with if you're new to crowning. A crown like this can be made with just chenille stems or wire of your choice, tape, and a few bunches of flowers with petite blooms. I chose to work with sweet autumn clematis. This prolific bloomer climbs up the doorway of my home every fall, releasing its delicious scent every time I brush past. Out of water the blooms are fleeting, so I pre-hydrate the cut flowers to lengthen the life of the crown. (See "Handling," page 20, in the "Tools and Techniques" section for more.) Other petite blooms that would look lovely and last much longer include chamomile, gypsophila, waxflower, statice, *Pieris japonica*, and astrantia.

MATERIALS:

- 2 white chenille stems
- About 120 individual clematis florets, trimmed to 3 in (7.5 cm) (if using a different flower, 3 full bunches should be sufficient)
- Stem wrap tape
- Head form (optional but recommended)
- Oasis floral adhesive (optional)

STEP 1: Secure the 2 chenille stems by twisting them tightly together (it's easiest to work with this crown base if you keep it open in one long length). Using you own head as a guide, test the base for size. Bring the two ends together behind your head and make sure you have an additional 1 in (2.5 cm) or so of length on either side. These ends will not be covered with flowers; they will be twisted together as a closure for the finished crown only once it's on the wearer's head.

STEP 2: Add the florets to the base in little bundles of 3 to 6 florets. Create the desired fullness by deciding the number of blooms per bundle. Starting at one end of the base, hold your first bundle against the chenille and secure with stem wrap tape. Pull the tape taut before looping it around the stems of the bundle; it sticks only when stretched. Loop the tape around the bundle and base to get started, using one thumb to firmly hold the three components in place. With your other hand, pull the tape taut and wrap it around the stems a few times, keeping maximum tension on the tape to ensure a secure lock.

STEP 3: Continue working your way along the length of the crown base, adding each bundle in the same direction and in line with the last. The bloom end of each new bundle will hide the stem end of the last. Keep the tension on the tape, pulling it downward to meet the stem ends of each new bundle before using it to secure them to the base. For a fuller result, place the bundles close together; for a more delicate look, space them out a bit. Make sure the crown has a front and back—when placed on the head, the blooms of the finished piece should all lie on the same plane, facing outward.

STEP 4: After the crown base is covered, except for the closure ends, place it on the head form or wearer's head to analyze the finished piece and tweak as desired.

STEP 5: Add more florets to the piece using floral adhesive. The strong structure that you created with the firmly taped bundles offers many reliable little nooks into which to tuck in additional florets.

STEP 6: Spray the crown with water and package it for storage or presentation.

DEMI-CROWN

Hand wiring can be laborious, but it is a fantastic floristry skill to master. Wiring each component gives designers much more control over the materials by enabling them to bend and manipulate each one. Adding wired stems to a crown base allows the designer to move them up, down, left, or right — creating a dynamic, multidimensional piece. I've used the skills outlined here to make many demi-crowns over the years. In this crown, the strong-stemmed artemisia are added as is; all the other components are wired, and the delicate pepperberry and tomatoes are attached to the finished piece with floral adhesive.

MATERIALS:

- 5 to 7 stems lisianthus 'Rosanne Brown'
- 1 stem white tuberose
- 2 or 3 stems blushing bride protea
- 1 large stem immature privet berry
- 5 to 7 stems buttercream scabiosa buds

- 2 or 3 stems artemisia 'Silver Queen'
- 1 large stem immature pepperberry
- 2 or 3 stems immature currant tomato
- 24-gauge straight floral wire
- Stem wrap tape

- Oasis floral adhesive
- Bobby pins

STEP 1: Cut all the floral materials, retaining a stem length of 1 to 2 in (2.5 to 5 cm).

STEP 2: Wire the lisianthus using the piercing method (see page 28). Insert the wire through the calyx until it's evenly centered, fold the two wire ends down alongside the short stem, and secure with stem wrap tape.

STEP 3: Wire the tuberose florets, protea, and privet using the cranking method (see page 28). Group 2 or 3 stems together and tape them snugly. The tape both locks them together and protects their delicate or fleshy stems from injury from the wire. To wire them, hold the taped florets in one hand, press the wire to the back of the bundle, and use the other hand to firmly crank it around the stem section of the bundle until secure. Fold the wire ends down and, pulling the tape taut, pull it down while twisting the wire to cover the wire ends completely.

STEP 4: Wire the scabiosa blooms using the insertion method (see page 28). Insert the wire end deep into the flower head (but not so far that it pops out of the face of the flower) alongside the stem and secure the stem and wire with stem wrap tape.

STEP 5: To prepare the base wire for the demi-crown, cut a 10 in (25 cm) length of floral wire and cover it completely with stem wrap tape. Form a small loop on either end and twist tightly to lock each in place. Press the stem wrap tape firmly against one end of the wire just below the loop, pull it taut, and wrap it around the base wire a few times, firmly locking the tape to the base.

STEP 6: Add the floral materials to the base, starting with tiny scabiosa buds, delicate artemisia sprigs, and small privet bundles. With each floral addition, pull the tape down to meet the stem of the flower and again wrap the tape around a few times to lock the stem to the base wire. Every few additions, move the base wire out of the way and trim away the excess wire tails of each floral component.

STEP 7: Continue adding materials, working your way up to larger florets, bending the wire as needed to face the bloom end of the flower out, away from the base wire. To create depth and dimension, place some floral components flush to the base wire and leave the wire on others longer, allowing them to float above the denser materials.

CONTINUED

STEP 8: Continue adding, alternating material type and orientation of the blooms. At the halfway point, focus on fullness with multiple florets of tuberose and the largest lisianthus blooms.

STEP 9: After attending to the fullest central area, work your way down the rest of the length of the crown to the end, placing the materials closer and tighter to the base wire and choosing smaller materials as you approach the end.

STEP 10: Complete the end of the piece by wiring the privet; it drapes well and can be bent back on itself so the tips of the florets face down at about a 45-degree angle. Add it snugly to the base and tape securely. This will start to cover the lower loop end of the demi-crown.

STEP 11: Using the floral adhesive, dip the stem ends of tiny sections of pepperberry, artemisia, and privet (similar to those wired in step 6) into the lower section of the crown, finding landing spots for the stems within the wired matrix of materials above. Finish the piece by using adhesive to add flourishes of pepperberry and currant tomatoes throughout.

STEP 12: Spray the crown with water, hook 2 bobby pins through each wired loop, and package it for storage or presentation.

FULL FLOWER CROWN

This is my favorite method for creating full, voluminous, over-the-top flower crowns. I wire all the floral components individually before taping them onto the strong base wire. The lisianthus and spray roses were wired using the piercing method; the feather celosia, artemisia, blueberry, privet, astrantia, didiscus, and oreganos were wired using the cranking method; and the scabiosa was wired using the insertion method (see page 28 for more information on these methods). The best (and most fun) part of this process is the embellishment stage. The strong crown structure created by wiring and taping each element provides many reliable nooks and crannies for tucking in these glued elements. After all the wired components are secured to the base, I love to glue in unexpected gestural or textural materials.

MATERIALS:

- 24-gauge floral wire

- 7 to 9 stems lisianthus 'Rosanne Brown'

- 2 or 3 stems spray rose 'Eloquence'

- 3 or 4 stems feather celosia (Celosia spicata)

- 1 or 2 stems immature blueberry

- 5 to 7 stems artemisia

- 3 to 5 stems immature privet berry

- 5 to 7 stems astrantia

- 7 to 9 stems scabiosa 'Black Knight'

- 5 to 7 stems heuchera foliage

- 7 to 9 stems didiscus

- 7 to 9 stems ornamental oregano 'Hopley's Purple'

- 7 to 9 stems ornamental oregano 'Kent Beauty'

- Oasis rustic wire

- Stem wrap tape

- Glass head form (optional, but recommended)

- Oasis floral adhesive

STEP 1: Using you own head as a guide, measure the wire to create the crown base. Bring the two ends together behind your head, making sure you have an additional 1 in (2.5 cm) or so of length on either side of the meeting point before cutting. These extra lengths will not be covered with flowers but twisted together as a closure for the finished crown.

STEP 2: Wire all the floral components except the heuchera, using the appropriate wiring method for each (see page 28). All of the components can be wired ahead of time.

STEP 3: To prepare the base wire for the crown, press the stem wrap tape to the base and wrap it around to firmly lock it in place before you begin adding floral components.

STEP 4: Begin adding the floral components, starting with the smallest or most tapered. Add flowers one at a time, and with each addition wrap firmly around its stem section. The bloom of each subsequent flower you add will conceal the taped end of the last.

STEP 5: Continue adding materials, working your way up to larger florets, bending the wire as needed to face the bloom end of the flower out, away from the base wire. To create depth and dimension, place some floral components flush to the base wire and leave the wire on others longer, allowing them to float above the denser materials.

STEP 6: Continue, alternating material type and orientation of the blooms. At the halfway point, focus on fullness, adding the largest lisianthus and spray rose blooms. You can also play with height by leaving more length on the wired stem. You can group colors and specific flowers, creating an impactful focal area, or alternate varieties evenly throughout the piece, creating a more uniform crown. If the extra wired ends of the floral components become too bulky, trim them as you go.

STEP 7: After attending to the fullest central area, work your way down the rest of the length of the crown. Place the materials closer and tighter to the base wire, choosing smaller materials as you go.

STEP 8: When you reach the very end of the piece, trim off the wire ends of the last floral components right below the taped binding point. This little taped nubbin will be concealed when the crown is wrapped and joined around the head.

STEP 9: Position the crown on the head form as you would like it to be worn and, using floral adhesive, add detail to the focal area. Glue delicate materials such as the heuchera foliage and tiny clusters of blueberry onto landing spots in the dense matrix of wiring. This is where you get to have fun! Glue delicate materials until you're happy with the crown.

STEP 10: Spray the crown with water and package it for storage or presentation.

FLORAL FASCINATOR

"Fascinator" is the term used to describe a class of highly decorative, petite hats typically worn at the dressiest of occasions. Because I work with ephemera instead of textiles, my fascinators require a base material that's waterproof and not too precious, as it will be completely covered with floral elements and likely worn only once. After much experimentation, I found the perfect bases: plastic skull caps meant for making carnival headdresses. The bases are large—completely covering the head and most of the face when put on—so they must be cut to size. The lightweight, rounded plastic of the cap hugs the curves of the head well, is comfortable to wear, and is strong enough to support the weight of fresh flowers.

MATERIALS:

- 1 plastic skull cap for fascinator base
- 24-gauge floral wire
- Stem wrap tape
- Waterproof tape
- 8 bobby pins
- Glass head form

- Oasis floral adhesive
- 3 to 5 stems hanging amaranthus
- 5 to 7 stems ranunculus
- 5 to 7 stems lisianthus 'Rosanne Brown'
- 3 to 5 stems didiscus buds

- 5 to 7 cup-and-saucer vine (*Cobaea scandens*) blooms
- 3 to 5 stems sweet autumn clematis vine

NOTE: I recommend making these floral toppers and those that follow in chapter 6 a day or two before they will be worn. If you're giving one to someone to wear immediately, package it for presentation. I present my delicate wearables in a 9 by 9 in (23 by 23 cm) paper box lined with a pillow of shredded paper.

STEP 1: To prepare the fascinator base, cut an ovoid shape out of the plastic skull cap approximately 6 in (15 cm) long by 4 in (10 cm) wide.

STEP 2: Cover the floral wires with the stem wrap tape. Adding this layer of tape will ease handling and manipulating the wires. Form a loop at each end of the wires, using the fascinator base as a measurement guide. Tape the wires in place using the waterproof tape. You will use these loops to pin the finished piece to the hair. Add 2 bobby pins to each wire loop.

STEP 3: Position the fascinator base on the head form as you envision it being worn. Tape the base to secure it in place. Don't worry about the messy appearance of the base at this stage; it will be entirely covered with flowers.

STEP 4: Add a fine layer of glue to the entire fascinator base. Squeeze out more adhesive, about a quarter-size dollop at a time, into a little bowl or scrap of cardboard.

STEP 5: Start to add materials to the base. Cut the amaranthus florets from their stems and add them to the bottom edge of the base, allowing them to cascade off the piece.

STEP 6: Trim the ranunculus flush and remove the sepals. Turn them over and add a dot of glue to each. Press them firmly onto the base, concealing it with a complete layer.

STEP 7: Cut the lisianthus stems, leaving a little length. Dip them in the adhesive and tuck them into the ranunculus layer, allowing them to float above.

STEP 8: Add delicate tendrils of amaranthus throughout the bottom section of the piece.

STEP 9: Add the didiscus buds to the front perimeter of the piece.

STEP 10: Glue in the cup-and-saucer blooms throughout the piece, choosing appropriate stem lengths to allow them to either cascade down or float over the other floral layers. The tight network of the ranunculus and lisianthus will allow you to tuck in these blooms securely throughout the piece.

STEP 11: Finish with the delicate clematis vine, gluing it throughout the piece to add movement and an airy quality.

STEP 12: To store this piece, spray with water, seal it inside an airtight plastic bag, and store in a cooler or refrigerator.

STEP 13: To wear the piece, pin it into the hair with the bobby pins. The first bobby pin goes through the loop and into the hair; the second crosses over the first, forming an "X" to lock it securely into place.

Floral headpieces are incredibly fun to dream up and create. My loves for fashion, hat design, and flowers really come together when I make these arrangements. I find the engineering stage of planning most satisfying, as the more complex pieces require all the floral design techniques I've gathered over the years to execute. Inspiration comes from many places—from the natural quality of the flowers I have in mind for a piece (Wraparound Floral Fascinator, page 167), from a period in history (Asymmetrical Floral Headdress, page 175), or from a specific fashion house (Dramatic Dome Hat, page 181). Although I've made many of these over the years, most were made for my own pleasure—to express my love for floral fashion—or as entries for design contests. I have had a few paid commissions; the most incredible one was an order for many over-the-top Marie Antoinette–style pieces to be worn by models at a fashionista's eightieth birthday party in Mexico City. This felt like a return on all the years of making these for myself in hopes of attracting such a commission. The following projects show a diverse selection of headpiece styles and techniques. Test, experiment, and combine these ideas to create the one-of-a-kind pieces you crave to see!

6 / HEADPIECES

WRAPAROUND FLORAL FASCINATOR

The inspiration to make this piece came from my love of vintage hats and my obsession with *Pieris japonica*. This spring bloomer is pure gold to a florist—its exquisite cascading shape, bell-shaped flowers, and strong branches make it a wonderful choice for all design applications. I chose to work with these blooms exclusively for this piece to really show off its natural beauty. Beyond the pieris, all you'll need to make this impressive fascinator are a plastic skull cap, Oasis floral adhesive, tape, and a bit of florist wire. If pieris is unavailable or out of season, you can use materials with a similar structure and form, such as spirea, kochia, veronica, acacia, or heather.

MATERIALS:

- 1 plastic skull cap
- Oasis waterproof tape
- Glass head form
- 24-gauge floral wire
- Stem wrap tape
- 2 or 3 full bunches *Pieris japonica*
- Oasis floral adhesive
- Bobby pins

STEP 1: Trace a large "C" shape on the plastic skull cap and cut it out.

STEP 2: Using the waterproof tape, secure the skull cap base to the head form in the intended wear position.

STEP 3: Cover the floral wires with stem wrap tape. Adding this slightly tacky tape will give them more "grab." You will use the wires to bobby pin the fascinator to the hair, so a nonslip surface is crucial.

STEP 4: Using waterproof tape, secure the taped floral wires to the fascinator base.

STEP 5: Starting at the front of the piece, attach 3 to 5 complete bloom heads with waterproof tape until you've created fullness in the front focal area of the fascinator.

STEP 6: Cut the remaining pieris strands from their clusters.

STEP 7: Add a fine layer of glue to the fascinator base, working on a few inches of surface area at a time.

STEP 8: Squeeze out more adhesive, about a quarter-size dollop at a time, into a little bowl or scrap of cardboard. Add individual strands of pieris, first dipping each into the glue, then attaching to the fascinator base. With each addition, press and hold the stem in place to ensure that it's locked securely in place. Position all the strands so they lie in the same direction to create an effortless visual flow.

STEP 9: Once the entire base is covered, add multiple additional floral layers to the piece, paying close attention to the front half of the piece.

STEP 10: Add final strands of pieris to the focal area, choosing the most beautiful blooms and positioning them within the existing floral layers to fill gaps, create fullness, and add volume to the focal area. Allow the strands to cascade gracefully.

STEP 11: To store this piece, spray with water, seal it inside an airtight plastic bag, and store in a cooler or refrigerator.

STEP 12: To wear the piece, pin it into the hair with the bobby pins. The first bobby pin secures the wire into the hair; the second crosses over the first, forming an "X" to lock it securely into place.

NATURAL HAIR (AMARANTHUS EXTENSIONS)

I adore amaranthus; the swingy pendulous blooms always remind me of my friend Fatou's gorgeous sons' dreadlocks. She tends their hair immaculately, her expert hands training each glossy lock to hang in perfect uniformity. They turn heads and garner compliments everywhere they go — a tad tiresome for them, I think, but inspiring to me! A bumper crop of 'Coral Fountain' and 'Green Cascade' amaranthus that I scored at my friend Adrienne's farm gave me all I needed to create this fantasy "natural hair" headpiece. This was a simple but time-consuming project, as each floret was added to the base individually — but totally worth it for the movement and dimension this created. This piece also dried beautifully; in fact, I still have it in my studio (now painted gold), many months after I made it.

MATERIALS:

- 1 plastic skull cap
- Oasis waterproof tape
- Glass head form
- Oasis floral adhesive
- 12 to 15 bunches hanging amaranthus

STEP 1: To prepare the skull cap, cut away the forehead section completely, round the corners on both sides, and trim away a few inches from the back. When done, the cap, now your fascinator base, will resemble an open-face motorcycle helmet. Use waterproof tape to secure the cap to the glass head form.

STEP 2: Add a fine layer of glue to the back of the fascinator base, working on an inch or so of surface area at a time. Squeeze out more glue, about a quarter-size dollop at a time, into a little bowl or scrap of cardboard. Dip each individual amaranthus strand into this glue reservoir before adding it to the base.

STEP 3: Add individual amaranthus florets to the base, working on 1 in (2.5 cm) strips at a time. Dip each floret into the glue reservoir, press against the base, and hold for 10 to 15 seconds to ensure it's fully adhered. After each row of amaranthus is secured, move up to the space just above, and add another fine layer of adhesive to the base before continuing. Work your way around the base, layer by layer. Continue until you've worked your way up to the ear level of the head form.

STEP 4: After reaching ear level, work first on one side of a defined center part, then on the other. Continue to add rows of amaranthus until you reach the central line at the top of the skull cap.

STEP 5: Create the "bangs" portion of the headpiece in the same fashion as the back, starting at the perimeter of the skull cap, securing one row of amaranthus at a time.

STEP 6: Now the fun part begins! Continue to glue in individual amaranthus strands throughout the piece until it's as full and fabulous as you wish. The floral adhesive is very strong and reliable—the strands you took care to lay down originally in meticulous rows are your foundation. You can glue hundreds of additional florets to these foundational strands, adding as much length and volume as you'd like.

STEP 7: To store the piece, spray it with water, seal it inside an airtight plastic bag, and store it in your cooler or refrigerator.

ASYMMETRICAL FLORAL HEADDRESS

In my fantasies, pieces like these would be worn often, beyond florist's photo shoots, fashion shows, and the occasional magazine cover. They'd be worn at weddings (and not just by brides); to the theater and galas (I'm dreaming of you, Met Gala); and in place of statement jewelry on the red carpet. For this project, I chose a pastel palette of pink, pearly beige, and mint green and was inspired (loosely) by the towering hairstyles and hair ornaments of the Victorian era. The fluffy, hearty amaranthus and hydrangea are the perfect materials to use to hide the internal structure of the headpiece. Lisianthus blooms work well in wearable work—their blooms, although delicate looking, are quite leathery and strong. These headpieces can be made in countless shapes, color combinations, and eras—the possibilities are truly endless.

MATERIALS:

- 1 plastic skull cap
- 18 in (45 cm) length Oasis florist netting or chicken wire
- 2 chenille stems
- Glass head form
- Oasis waterproof tape
- 5 to 7 stems hanging amaranthus 'Autumn's Touch'
- 3 to 5 stems dried *Hydrangea paniculata* 'Strawberry Shake'
- Oasis floral adhesive
- 7 to 9 stems carnation 'Putumayo Beige'
- 5 to 7 stems snowberry (*symphoricarpos*)
- 3 to 5 stems *Pieris japonica*
- 5 to 7 stems peach lisianthus
- 3 to 5 stems spray rose 'Earth'
- 4 or 5 stems begonia foliage
- Water tubes
- 5 to 7 stems spray rose 'Natasha'
- 7 to 9 stems pale pink sweet pea
- 7 to 9 stems butterfly ranunculus 'Ariadne'
- Alligator hair clips (recommended for wear)

NOTE: When designing headpieces, take care to balance the weight of the piece appropriately, distributing the weight of the materials evenly on both sides.

STEP 1: Create the base by tracing a line around the crown of the skull cap, creating an ovoid shape, and cut it out.

STEP 2: Roll the netting into a multi-layered tubular cone shape, one end tighter than the other.

STEP 3: Punch four holes in the top of the skull cap, a pair on either side. Form a "U" shape with the chenille stems, and feed them through each pair of holes, approaching from underneath the cap. Pull the ends through the holes and twist a few times to lock the stems in place on the top of the cap. Secure the headpiece base to the head form with the waterproof tape.

STEP 4: Feed the netting cone onto the chenille stems, pulling it snug to the skull cap and twisting the chenille stems to secure it in place. This cone is the structure to which you will add most of the flowers, so be sure it's firmly affixed to the skull cap. Use your hands to bend and form the wire cone into a slight "S" shape with a high and low side.

STEP 5: Add the base layer materials, beginning with the hanging amaranthus and hydrangea. Weave their stems through a number of the holes in the netting until the stems are secured within the structure. When they feel snug, add a dot of floral adhesive to each stem to anchor. Let the amaranthus cascade down on the low side of the piece; on the high side, attach them more tightly to cover the wire cone. Work the hydrangea throughout to provide texture and coverage.

STEP 6: Continue adding base layer materials to cover the inner workings, next adding the carnations. These, like the amaranthus and leathery dried hydrangea, will look beautiful for days without a water source. As always when working with glue, have handy a glue reservoir in a little bowl or scrap of cardboard for easy application. Trim each carnation stem to about 2 in (5 cm) long, dip in the glue reservoir, and insert into a secure nook within the wire structure. Grouping the carnations in the central "valley" of the piece provides both beautiful color and a "pillow" for the more special flowers to float over.

STEP 7: Begin to add the textural snowberries and pieris. The snowberry lends a beautiful draping character to the low side of the piece, following the line created by the hanging amaranthus. Add a number of short stems directly to the headpiece base to cover the forwardmost portion of the base on the right side. Add a bit of snowberry to the left side of the piece to create a continuity and flow of materials throughout. Use the pieris similarly, to make an impact on the right and accent on the left.

STEP 8: Add the lisianthus by dipping their stems into the glue reservoir and tucking them into the left side of the piece. Display the bell-shaped blooms upside down to show off the subtle transition from buttercream to pale pink.

CONTINUED

STEP 9: Add multiple 'Earth' spray roses throughout the cone structure. Choose tightly closed buds, which will keep well without a water source.

STEP 10: Continue with the showy begonia foliage. Trim the leaves off their stems, dip each into the glue reservoir, and add them into the piece. Concentrate them in the very front so they can spill over the front edge of the piece, creating a subtle veil effect.

STEP 11: Begin adding the delicate blooms. These will need a water source to last the length of an event, so tuck the stems into water tubes before adding. Add the 'Natasha' spray roses first, leaving some long to add drama to the high side of the piece, others shorter to add throughout the rest of the piece. Tuck each water tube into the structure of the piece until you find a secure landing place. Add a little glue as needed if any of the tubes feel wiggly.

STEP 12: Continue with the sweet pea. Because they are slim, you can add multiple blooms to a single water tube. Find a safe nook in the high side of the piece to tuck these into.

STEP 13: Finish with the butterfly ranunculus, also equipped with water tubes. Add them throughout the piece, to cascade gently over the high side and to add finish to the forwardmost focal area.

STEP 14: To store this piece, spray the with water, seal it inside an airtight plastic bag, and store in your cooler or refrigerator. A piece this large is difficult to transport; I recommend leaving it on the head form, packing it in a sturdy low box, securing it with packing material, and covering the entire piece with plastic. Although the piece was designed to balance comfortably on the head, it's wise to include alligator clips (available at salon supply stores) that can be used to attach it into the wearer's hair. Wire loops for bobby pins can also be added to the piece (see page 160 for detailed instructions).

DRAMATIC DOME HAT

A few years ago, an outing to Detroit Garden Works (one of my favorite garden centers, and a must if you find yourself in Detroit) produced many treasures, including a collection of stiff dome-shaped papier-mâché pot liners. I used the largest one to create a Dior-inspired electric-blue dome hat encased in blue delphinium florets. The hat won gold in an international floral design contest—a real thrill! But more satisfying to me was how easy the hat was to make. A few years later I was inspired to re-create the dome hat, making my own hat base using Mod Podge, craft paper, and a large bowl. This time, instead of delphinium, I chose white larkspur to pair with a fantastic '60s-inspired pearl-embellished two-piece dress.

MATERIALS:

- Large bowl or a large round balloon
- Plastic wrap
- Scotch tape
- Mod Podge craft glue
- Craft paper (or another inexpensive paper, thicker than printer paper), cut into 500 to 600 manageable strips

- Foam brush
- 2 small bowls to use for both glue types
- Wide wired ribbon
- Hot glue gun

- 8 to 10 bunches white larkspur or delphinium
- Oasis floral adhesive
- Glass head form

STEP 1: Prepare the bowl for Mod Podge application by covering it with long lengths of plastic wrap, flipping it upside down, and taping each piece snugly into the inside of the bowl. Be sure to cover the bowl completely.

STEP 2: Pour the Mod Podge into a little bowl. Consult the Mod Podge bottle for more details on application and drying time between layers. To create the hat base, apply the paper strips to the bowl, using the Mod Podge. Brush the glue onto the bowl surface using the foam brush, and smooth the paper onto the glued area by brushing the paper with a top coat of Mod Podge. Work your way across the surface of the bowl, completing one long row at a time before starting the next.

STEP 3: Cover the bowl form with three complete layers. Allow to dry overnight.

STEP 4: Remove the dried hat base from the bowl by simply releasing the taped plastic wrap and pulling to separate the bowl from the hat base. Discard the plastic wrap or save for another project.

STEP 5: To make the hat band, which adds inner structure to the dome hat, measure and cut the wired ribbon, using your own head as a gauge. Glue the ends together using the hot glue gun.

STEP 6: Place the hat band inside the center of the hat base, using hot glue to secure it in place.

STEP 7: Cut the larkspur florets from their stems and place them in a bowl. Squeeze out a pool of floral adhesive into another bowl and keep both close.

STEP 8: Begin with the inside of the hat base. Dip individual florets of larkspur into the floral adhesive and press them onto the hat form. Start by placing them snugly against the hat band. After you complete a full circle, start another—right next to the last—working in concentric rows until the entire underside of the hat is fully covered in florets. Pay close attention to the last several rows and the lower edge of the hat form—these will be especially visible when the hat is worn. Add extra florets as needed to fill holes or even out the contours of the hat base.

STEP 9: Flip the hat base over, and place on the head form. The exterior surface of the hat base needs to be treated a little differently than the interior. Gravity is working against you on this side of the piece. To combat this, add a fine layer of glue to the hat base before pressing each glued floret into place—the glue-to-glue placement will ensure a strong bond.

STEP 10: Perfect the base by adding florets throughout, paying special attention to the outer edge of the hat. Step back often and analyze the contours of the piece, adding florets as necessary to perfect the domed form.

STEP 11: To store the piece, spray it with water, seal it inside an airtight plastic bag, and store it in your cooler or refrigerator. Inspect the piece before wear, as some of the florets may shrink a tad during storage. Add new florets as necessary. A piece this large is difficult to transport. I recommend leaving it on the head form, packing it into a sturdy low box, securing it with packing material, and covering the entire piece with plastic.

FLOWER 'FRO

Several years ago, I saw an image of a man with a full, bushy beard in which cotinus fluff had been artfully arranged. He was the husband of the wonderfully talented florist Sarah Winward, and she was the artful arranger. It occurred to me that if huge handfuls of flowers could be held by the structure of a small beard, so much more could be held in a full head of hair. The flower 'fro was born out of pure curiosity and play. For those not born with hair they can grow into an afro, or for long or demanding events, a good-quality afro wig can be used. The benefit of using a wig is that materials can be glued directly into the hair of the wig for a very solid, long-lasting design.

MATERIALS:

FOR THE CROWN:

- 24-gauge floral wire
- 7 to 9 stems lisianthus 'Rosanne Brown'
- 9 to 12 stems carnation 'Putumayo Beige'
- 7 to 9 stems blushing bride protea
- 7 to 9 stems immature currant tomatoes
- 12 to 15 stems artemisia
- 3 to 5 stems immature privet berry
- 5 to 7 stems amaranthus 'Hot Biscuits'

- 12 to 15 stems ornamental oregano 'Hopley's Purple'
- 2 full bunches asparagus fern
- 7 to 9 stems white scabiosa
- 7 to 9 stems peach tower asters
- Design Master Uber matte paint in Crema
- Oasis rustic wire
- Stem wrap tape
- Glass head form (optional, but recommended)

FOR THE 'FRO:

- 2 bunches plumosus fern
- Design Master Uber matte paint in Crema
- 12 to 15 stems artemisia
- 12 to 15 stems ornamental oregano 'Hopley's Purple'
- 7 to 9 stems carnation 'Putumayo Beige'
- 3 to 5 stems lisianthus 'Rosanne Brown'

STEP 1: First create a full, wired flower crown, referencing the technique used for "Full Flower Crown" (page 155). Use the piercing method for the lisianthus and carnation. For the blushing bride protea, tomatoes, artemisia, privet, amaranthus, oregano, and fern, use the cranking method. And use the insertion method for the scabiosa and tower asters.

STEP 2: Secure the crown on your model's head as snugly as is comfortable.

STEP 3: Next, create the 'fro. Spray the plumosus fern with the paint and allow them to dry. Cut the plumosus fern into manageable lengths, 4 to 7 in (10 to 17 cm). (Leave enough for steps 5 and 7.) Tuck the stems underneath the back of the crown, allowing the foliage to fall over the rest of the hair. Continue to add lengths, tucking their stems and guiding their tips to cover the back of the head. Dainty pieces can be inserted directly into the hair, while heavier stems will need the structure of the crown as an anchor.

STEP 4: Continue with the artemisia, adding the long delicate lengths into the crown structure and allowing the foliage end to trail out at the back of the head.

STEP 5: Work your way around the back of the head, adding ornamental oregano and additional plumosus and artemisia. Anchor stem ends anywhere in the entire crown structure. Weave foliage tips into the hair as necessary to secure.

STEP 6: Add carnations and lisianthus to the forwardmost top portion of the head by tucking their stems into the crown, the most reliable position to secure these heavy stems.

STEP 7: Add additional fern throughout to perfect the form of the piece, and trim out any distracting materials.

STEP 8: This design is wearable and functional as "hair," but within reason—instruct the wearer to take care as she navigates her event. I wouldn't recommend jumping on a trampoline or riding a motorcycle while modeling your flower 'fro.

I think of myself as a floral accessory designer, so for me, "floral fashion" doesn't mean an entire dress of flowers or an over-the-top, head-to-toe composition. I delight in making floral wearables that pique interest and grab attention but are accessible and relatively salable and can be made in a single workday. In this chapter you will find a variety of floral fashion designs ranging from simple to complex, petite to grand. I'm thrilled to share some of my favorite concepts; I encourage you to borrow from these ideas, combine them, and allow them to inspire your own unique looks.

7 / FLORAL FASHION

FLORAL BUSTIER

The idea for this carnation petal bustier was loosely inspired by the incredible couture designer Krikor Jabotian. I happened upon a particularly beautiful photo of his work—an intricately ruffled, multidimensional construction of fabric petals arranged on a brocade bodice—and it sparked my imagination. I used a purchased bustier as the base for this design and created the asymmetrical shoulder portion of the bustier out of craft foam, then sewed that to the bodice. This design took me 6½ hours to make, using an estimated 2,660 carnation petals. The leathery durability of the carnations made them the perfect choice for such a time-consuming piece.

MATERIALS:

- 125 to 135 stems standard carnation
- Faux leather fabric
- Two ¹⁄₁₆ in (2 mm) white craft foam sheets
- Hot glue gun
- Bustier with foam breast cups and boning structure
- Dress form or tabletop mannequin
- Fishing line or strong thread
- Large upholstery sewing needle
- Clear packing tape
- Oasis floral adhesive

STEP 1: Cut the carnation calyxes, freeing the individual petals. You can cut them ahead of time or as you work.

STEP 2: Cut a 10 by 3 in (25 by 7.5 cm) oval out of the faux leather as the base for the craft foam part of the design.

STEP 3: Sketch ovoid shapes of various sizes on the craft foam. This is where you can have fun and experiment. The shapes don't need to be perfect, as they'll be covered entirely with carnation petals. Aim for 10 to 15 ovals, ranging in size from 4½ to 6½ in (11 to 16.5 cm) long and 3 to 3½ in (7.5 to 9 cm) wide. Cut them out.

STEP 4: Roll each craft foam oval to form a little cone. Hot glue the seam of the cone to secure.

STEP 5: Place the bustier on the dress form and snap it into place.

STEP 6: Tape the faux leather platform for the shoulder piece to the form to keep it in place while you're attaching it. Either affix it to the bustier using hot glue, or, if you want to use the bustier for a future project, sew it to the bustier using fishing line or a heavy-duty thread.

STEP 7: Add the cones to the faux leather base using hot glue. Press and hold each cone in place until the glue sets. Work your way down the faux leather base, staggering and alternating direction with each cone. In addition to gluing the cones to the faux leather base, also glue them to each other. Add any additional cones to fill out the design as desired.

STEP 8: Cover the entire bustier with clear packing tape. This will protect the surface of the bustier so it can be used again and also provide a more reliable surface for the petals to adhere to. If the tape feels insecure, unsnap the bustier and, working with long lengths of tape, wrap the entire inside and outside of the bustier.

STEP 9: Trace a line with floral glue to the exterior perimeter of the highest cone. Press individual carnation petals to the glued area, making sure each is adhered. In addition to adding glue to the cone, you can add some to each petal for added strength. Work your way around the entire cone, row by row, before moving on to the next cone.

CONTINUED

STEP 10: After the shoulder portion of the bustier is complete, move on to the breast cups. Trace a fine line of floral glue on the top edge of the cup and attach individual petals, pressing each in place for a few seconds. Work across the entire contour of the cup, then add another line of adhesive and start another row of petals underneath the first. With each row, pay attention to the contour of the area and shorten your rows appropriately to trace the line of the breast cup.

STEP 11: Trace a fine line of glue across the entire trunk of the bustier. Place petals in uniform rows, working your way across the torso area. Continue until the entire bustier is covered with neat rows of petals.

STEP 12: For added visual interest and to break up the uniform rows of petals on the torso, add a cascade of petals starting from the top of the torso all the way to the bottom.

STEP 13: Once the bodice is completely covered, consider gluing on individual petals to cover any problem spots or to add more movement to the shoulder portion of the design.

STEP 14: Spray the completed piece thoroughly with water, cover with a plastic bag, and store in your cooler or a dark cold place.

FLORAL
EPAULETTES

The word "epaulette" comes from *epaule*, the French word for shoulder.
Traditionally, epaulettes are shoulder decorations worn by the military,
used to show rank. In fashion, epaulettes are ornamental pieces that flat-
ter the lovely collarbone area and draw the attention upward, framing the
face. Even though the flower choices in this design are soft and delicate,
the design still communicates strength and confidence.

MATERIALS:

- Faux leather fabric
- Hot glue gun
- Waterproof kinesiology tape with paper backing
- Corsage pins (optional)
- Tabletop mannequin or dress form
- Oasis floral adhesive
- 2 stems blue hybrid delphinium
- 10 to 12 stems blue muscari
- 5 to 7 stems white astrantia
- 5 to 7 stems ornamental onion (*Allium cowanii*)
- 7 to 9 stems star of Bethlehem (*Ornithogalum arabicum*)
- 8 to 10 stems snowdrop

STEP 1: Create the shoulder pad platforms for the epaulettes using faux leather fabric. Sketch two ovals, 6½ in (16.5 cm) long by 4½ in (11 cm) wide, and cut them out.

STEP 2: Cut a 3 in (7.5 cm) slit in each oval. Add hot glue to the edge of one half of the slit, bring it over the other, and press it down, forming a dart. This gives the ovals a rounded shape, allowing them to hug the shoulders.

STEP 3: On the faux leather fabric, trace a slightly rounded strip, 1 in (2.5 cm) wide by 12 in (30.5 cm) long, and cut it out. This strap will connect the shoulder pieces, spanning the upper back and attaching to the shoulder pieces on either side.

STEP 4: Hot glue a piece of kinesiology tape to the underside of each oval. If the finished epaulettes will be worn on top of the fabric of a dress or jacket, you can use corsage pins instead of tape to keep them in place.

STEP 5: Place the ovals on the mannequin, with the rounded dart side facing away from the body, and tape them down with waterproof tape.

STEP 6: Glue the ends of the faux leather strap to the ovals using hot glue.

STEP 7: Start with the delphinium florets, adding a bit of floral glue to each bloom's underside and pressing it into place on the shoulder pad. Using many florets creates a base layer for the design.

STEP 8: Add the muscari, dipping the stems in glue and attaching to the lower edge of the design, allowing them to cascade down.

STEP 9: Add the astrantia florets, dipping each in glue before pressing it into place, clustered around the delphinium florets.

STEP 10: Cut the allium flower heads from their stems, add glue to the base of each, and press them into place. Face some upward for volume and others on their sides.

STEP 11: Add the ornithogalum florets. Cut them from the bloom head, add a bit of glue to each tip, and add them to the design. To increase their impact, cluster them in groupings of 3 to 5.

STEP 12: With the base mostly covered, add the snowdrops, cascading some off of the base and gluing others upright to show off their lovely nodding arc shape.

STEP 13: Perfect the design, adding additional blooms to cover any gaps. Stand up a few tiny muscari stems to replicate how they grow in nature.

STEP 14: After fully decorating both shoulders, cover the neck strap with the most durable flowers, the delphinium and astrantia.

FLEXIBLE FASHION

This project is one of my favorite floral wearable methods to share. Although it's a relatively simple idea, the flexibility and wearability of this piece makes it very useful to have in a designer's toolbox. I love that this one piece can be worn four (or more!) ways. I remember a photo shoot a few years back; I was on set with this book's photographer, Amanda Dumouchelle, and she kept positioning this piece on our model in different ways. We liked each new position more than the last and were excited by the ease and adaptability of the design. In addition to a necklace, belt, crown, and corsage, this concept can also be adapted to make a floral dog collar, hat band, sash, or necktie. I love the ribbons from May Arts (see "Resources," page 218).

MATERIALS:

- Faux leather fabric
- Eyelet kit
- Silk ribbon
- Oasis floral adhesive
- Spartan brand kinesiology tape with paper backing
- 3 to 5 stems pale yellow ranunculus

- 3 to 5 stems white star carnation
- 1 or 2 stems white strawflower
- 2 or 3 stems bleached, preserved ruscus

- 2 or 3 stems ornamental onion (*Allium cowanii*)
- 2 or 3 stems peach hypericum
- 2 or 3 stems white astrantia

STEP 1: Sketch an ovoid shape, 10½ in (26.5 cm) long by 3 in (7.5 cm) wide, on the faux leather fabric.

STEP 2: Cut out the oval and install an eyelet at either end.

STEP 3: Measure two 1 yd (91 cm) lengths of ribbon and feed them through the eyelets. These will allow the piece to be worn as a crown, belt, or necklace.

STEP 4: If you'd like the piece to be wearable as a shoulder corsage on a bare shoulder, flip the platform over and glue an appropriately sized strip of kinesiology tape to the back. (For more on how to instead use pins to attach the piece to clothing, see "Shoulder Corsage" on page 107.)

STEP 5: Add a fine layer of glue to the platform and squeeze a small amount into a bowl.

STEP 6: Starting with the ranunculus— the largest flowers—cut the stems flush, add a bit of glue to the back, and press them onto the base.

STEP 7: Continue with the star carnation, dipping each stem into the glue reservoir before pressing it onto the base.

STEP 8: Add the strawflowers, nestling them in next to the ranunculus.

STEP 9: Distribute the more delicate materials—the bleached ruscus, allium, hypericum, and astrantia—throughout the piece, creating texture and movement. Pay attention to depth—place larger elements flush to the base and let lighter, airier elements float over them.

STEP 10: Analyze the piece, lifting it off the work surface and rounding it out in your hand (or trying it on), to be sure the entire base is concealed.

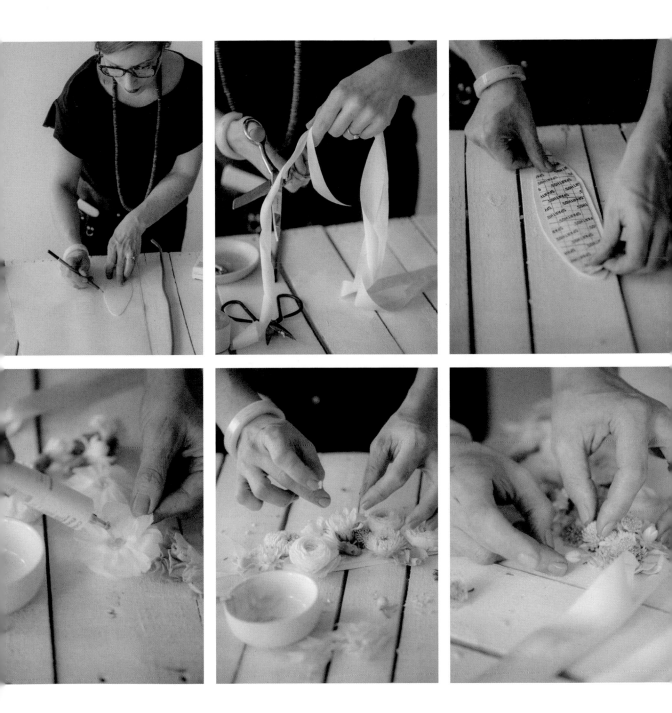

ROSY SHRUG

The 'Toffee' and 'Cappuccino' roses that I've been obsessing over lately definitely inspired this design. Their unexpected and otherworldly color and the soft, suede-like quality of their ruffled petals remind me of thick satin fabric. These qualities inspired me to make this fluffy floral shrug. The design looks impressive but is actually very simple and easy to create. The 'Cappuccino' roses' soft shade and smaller bloom size make them the perfect flower to float over the 'Toffee' roses, adding more interest and dimension to the piece. I can see this head-turning accessory worn by a fashion-forward bride or to a gala or fashion show by an adventurous flower lover.

MATERIALS:

- Faux leather fabric
- Dress form or tabletop mannequin (optional)
- 35 to 45 stems rose 'Toffee'
- Oasis floral adhesive
- 5 to 7 stems rose 'Cappuccino'
- 5 to 7 stems double peach lisianthus

STEP 1: To create the base for the shrug, sketch your own base on pattern paper or scrap packing paper. Test your pattern on yourself or on a mannequin or dress form. Trim as needed to create a C-shaped shrug base that drapes on the body with ease. Trace the shape of your tested pattern onto the faux leather fabric and cut out.

STEP 2: Cut several of the 'Toffee' roses flush and cut the rest, leaving a few inches of stem on most and longer stems on a few for the shoulder section.

STEP 3: Add a generous layer of glue to the shrug base and the backs of the 'Toffee' roses. Wait 15 to 20 seconds to allow the adhesive to get tacky.

STEP 4: Press the 'Toffee' roses onto the shrug base, nestling them close together. Press and hold each down for 15 to 20 seconds to be sure it is securely attached.

STEP 5: Working your way around the entire base, cover it completely with 'Toffee' roses.

STEP 6: Add the reserved stemmed 'Toffee' roses for increased depth and dimension. Dip them into the floral adhesive and tuck them into the piece, choosing secure spots in the design. Add the longest-stemmed roses to the shoulder section to create fullness and a nice rounded shape.

STEP 7: Add the 'Cappuccino' roses, clustering several on one shoulder to create a lovely focal point, and placing a few on the opposite shoulder as a smaller "echo."

STEP 8: Finish with the peach lisianthus, tucking their ruffled blooms into focal areas to accentuate the 'Cappuccino' roses.

FLORAL AURA

The idea for this piece came to me years ago, during a sketching session. I loved the idea of encasing the human form in an ethereal landscape of delicate flowers, but at the time I wasn't quite sure how I could do this. I recently revisited the old sketchbook and I knew I wanted to create this piece, and I knew how! I combined a wired crown with two long floral tattoos. I chose a mix of delicate yellow and white flowers for this design, because I wanted the piece to look light and airy. After a little light research on auras, I discovered that yellow auras symbolize creativity, awakening, and inspiration.

MATERIALS:

- 24-gauge floral wire
- 5 to 7 stems blooming feather acacia
- 12 to 15 stems spray rose 'Earth'
- 10 to 12 stems pale yellow ranunculus
- 10 to 12 stems feverfew
- 5 to 7 stems rose sumac
- 10 to 12 stems white star carnation
- 7 to 10 stems pale yellow carnation
- 10 stems white lilac

- 1 metal headband
- Glass head form
- 12 to 15 stems paperwhite narcissus
- 10 to 12 stems yellow butterfly ranunculus
- Oasis floral adhesive
- Rubbing alcohol or other astringent
- Waterproof kinesiology tape
- 10 to 12 stems white strawflower
- 5 to 7 stems white astrantia

- 7 to 10 stems white gomphrena
- 5 to 7 stems narcissus
- 10 to 15 stems clematis seed heads
- 10 to 15 stems white agapanthus
- 1 white begonia plant

STEP 1: Create an intricate wired crown using some of the acacia, the spray roses, some of the pale yellow ranunculus, feverfew, rose sumac, star carnation, pale yellow carnation petals, and lilac. (For detailed instructions on wiring, see "Wiring Techniques" on page 28. For a detailed crown tutorial, see "Full Flower Crown" on page 155.)

STEP 2: Use 24-gauge floral wire to secure the wired flower crown to the headband base.

STEP 3: Place the crown on your head form.

STEP 4: Insert appropriate lengths of floral wire into the stems of a few of the paperwhites and the butterfly ranunculus to strengthen their stems and prevent wilting. Trim any excess wire, and dip each stem in floral adhesive before tucking them into the wired structure of the crown.

STEP 5: Prepare for applying the floral tattoos by cleansing the skin with alcohol and allow to dry.

STEP 6: Tear the kinesiology tape into manageable lengths and press it onto the skin, tracing a line from the base of the ear down to the fingertip on both sides of the body.

STEP 7: Prepare the flowers by trimming them to size. Cut the strawflower, pale yellow ranunculus, astrantia, gomphrena, feverfew, and some of the narcissus flush, and trim the rest of the materials, retaining a bit of stem length.

STEP 8: Squeeze a small amount of floral adhesive into a bowl. The flowers are added in layers, from heaviest and largest to lightest and smallest. You can work on one side of the body first, or add each floral layer to both sides—this is more likely to give you a balanced result. Start with the largest flowers, the ranunculus. Consider the most flattering placement for the largest blooms; the ridge of the shoulder and upper arm are good places to cluster them. Add tiny dots of glue where you'd like to place these.

STEP 9: Add a dot of glue to the back of each ranunculus. Wait a moment for the glue to get tacky, then press each flower onto the tape. Hold each bloom down firmly for 10 to 15 seconds to secure it to the tape.

STEP 10: To add the strawflowers, add dots of glue to the tape and to the underside of each bloom, press the two together, and hold until they are secured in place.

CONTINUED

STEP 11: Add the acacia florets in the same way. These aren't the next in line size-wise, but they will cascade off the tape and help to conceal the mechanics, so they are best added now before the smaller and more delicate flowers.

STEP 12: Add the remaining gomphrena, feverfew, astrantia, and paperwhite, and the clematis. Dip them into the glue reservoir or add a small dot of glue to each before pressing them into place. These light, petite flowers need a little less adhesive to attach securely.

STEP 13: Finish with the most delicate materials—the agapanthus florets, begonia, individual paperwhite blooms, and star carnation petals.

STEP 14: Place the crown on the head and inspect the entire design. Add any necessary materials to join the crown piece to the neck portion of the tattoo on both sides of the body to create one cohesive, continuous-looking design.

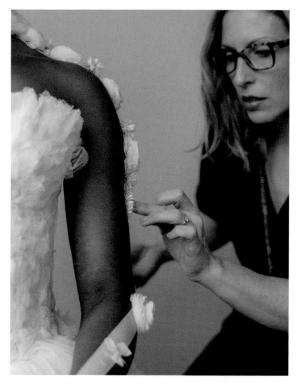

ACKNOWLEDGMENTS

Writing a book has been a dream of mine for years, and I'm incredibly humbled and grateful that the opportunity arose so effortlessly. I have many people to thank for this; first, my parents, Elizabeth and Richard McLeary. Their curiosity, love of books, appreciation for the natural world, and the value they placed on the handmade and the well designed set the stage for me to grow into the designer and author I am today. To my husband, Chaad, and children, Leda and Maceo—this book would not have been possible without their patience and support. The kids aren't quite sure what the big deal is about now, but I trust they'll enjoy this book thoroughly later in life. Special thanks to Chaad, and to my sister Erin, for their patience with me as I forced them to help me better articulate a particularly difficult section. The satisfaction I feel now, having successfully transferred my design process to the page, is due to their ability to translate my anxious abstractions into human words. To my husband's wonderful family, the Thomases, especially Nola, Ervin, and Chiara, who have encouraged me and expressed their heartfelt pride in my efforts since day one. To my dear friend and mentor, Holly Chapple, and the entire Chapel Designer family, who influenced me greatly, showing me that one's passion must be their life's work, and that large dreams are absolutely attainable. I heard each word of encouragement, and drew courage from them all—thank you. To my Detroit "flower friends," Lisa, Liz, Jody, and Heather—true friends who listen, encourage, balance, and inspire—thank you all for your enthusiasm, humor, and soul-lifting sisterhood. To the "Zanziladies," Carolyn, Maureen, Chelsy, Amanda, and Melissa—thank you all for the comic relief, the delicious dinners, and friendship during this process. Special thanks to Amanda Dumouchelle, the photographer who really inspired me to put my work out into the world. Her work elevates mine, and for that I am truly grateful. She put countless hours into this project, and did so with patience, enthusiasm, and balance. I'm indebted to her for her friendship and dedication. To Debra Prinzing, for her insight, encouragement, and advice. She is a true gem to the industry to whom I look often for inspiration. Heartfelt thanks to Françoise Weeks, who showed me (just by being herself) that a career as a floral artist is a real possibility. Her unwavering dedication to her craft has been a wonderful example to me.

Thank you to Julia Marie Schmitt, AIFD, EMC, and Joseph Massie—I am grateful for their honest review of the design process portion of this book and for what I've learned from them over the years. I greatly admire the command of their craft that they both hold. I strive to understand and explain our art as clearly and beautifully as they do.

A special thanks to Florabundance, for providing many of the gorgeous flowers and foliage seen in this book.

To the president of Florabundance, Joost Bongaerts, for his trust and support in this project, and to my wonderfully talented salesperson, Jose Rabelo, for his responsiveness, patience, and wonderful eye for selecting the perfect materials.

A warm thank you to Adrianne Gammie of Marilla Field and Flower for welcoming me to her flower field with little notice and allowing me to scoop up all the hanging amaranthus—as well as countless other little gems. These locally grown beauties added sparkle and a sense of place to the work. My heart bursts with gratitude to Rachel Hiles and the Chronicle Books team for choosing me to be the designer for this project. I'm thankful that this dream project found me and that I was prepared to accept the challenge.

Thank you to the numerous enthusiastic friends who enquired, encouraged, and urged me on—either by example or outright cheering—including Abby Olitzky, Heather Leavitt, Diana Marsh, Erin Benzakein, Sue Prutting, Nina Foster, Becca Blue, and Tobey Nelson.

To my agents, Leslie Jonath and Leslie Stoker, for the calm, encouraging way they led me through this process. Thank you to all the wonderful models who brought the pieces in this book to life. A special thanks to our lead model, LaPorcshia Winfield, for her patience, grace, and intoxicating talent. Thank you to the makeup artists for this project, the kind and wonderful Esther Soto and Hannah Butler. Last but not least, to the many, many kind people who encouraged me along the way on my social channels—your kind words have given me strength! Thank you all.

RESOURCES

BHLDN

www.bhldn.com

Source for fashion-forward special event wear at an accessible price.

Claire's

www.claires.com

Affordable fashion jewelry and accessories, including metal headbands.

Dutch Flower Line

www.dutchflowerline.com

Incredible selection of the finest quality cut flowers. New York City based, flowers shipped throughout the United States.

Florabundance

www.florabundance.com

Go-to floral wholesaler for flowers, foliage, and herbs. Wonderful selection and excellent customer service. Large selection of seasonal and domestically grown materials. California based, flowers shipped throughout the United States.

Forever 21

www.forever21.com

Source for affordable jewelry and accessories.

Green Paper Products

www.greenpaperproducts.com

Resource for biodegradable plastic packaging.

Jans Jewels

www.jansjewels.com

Go-to resource for brass cuff bracelet, necklace, and earring blanks.

Joann Fabrics

www.joann.com

Source for faux leather fabric, Mod Podge, chenille stems, and eyelet kit.

Marilla Field and Flora

www.marillafield.com

Local resource for many of the gorgeous flowers seen in these pages.

May Arts

www.mayarts.com

Wholesale ribbon supplier. Wide selection of high-quality silk ribbons at an affordable price.

Oasis Floral Products

www.oasisfloralproducts.com

Resource for rustic wire, bullion wire, jewelry wire, waterproof tape, stem wrap tape, hydrating solutions, finishing spray, and the essential floral adhesive.

Paper Mart

www.papermart.com

Resource for packaging and presentation. Craft paper boxes, shredded paper, and drawstring linen bags.

Rent the Runway

www.renttherunway.com

Thousands of rental designer clothing pieces, from blouses to ballgowns. Wonderful, easy-to-use resource for photo shoots or events.

Rings & Things

www.rings-things.com

Source for jewelry-making supplies, tools, and bezel cup ring blanks.

Save On Crafts

www.save-on-crafts.com

Hobbyist's resource for floral and crafting supplies.

Slow Flowers

www.slowflowers.com

Online directory and resource that serves to connect flower lovers to flower growers. Find local sources for cut flowers throughout the United States.

Spartan Tape

www.spartantape.rocks

Source for waterproof kinesiology tape with a paper backing.

Syndicate Sales

www.syndicatesales.com

Supply resource for water tubes, corsage supplies, florist netting, and florist wire.

Target

www.target.com

Source for 3M Nexcare tape and Elmer's glue.

Zucker Feather Products

www.zuckerfeather.com

The leading wholesale supplier of feather products for art, crafts, and costumes; some products are available through Amazon and Walmart.

INDEX